One spark can make a forest fire. One spark of pure Truth can set the world alight with Understanding of all things.

What is contained in this book can be that spark, for it brings Wisdom from *outside* of this Universe of yours, to bear on the real-life problems of Mankind.

Knowledge of eradicating *all* the illnesses and disorders of Man, quickly and simply, is contained within. Illnesses of body and troubles of mind. Knowledge of the World and Universe around you. Knowledge of other Universes and the Beings who inhabit them.

It brings you knowledge of the Aliens who walk among you now, whom you do not recognise – as yet.

The Being from the Core of All Power and Intelligence enlightens you on how to use Pure Thought, and contact your own Higher Intelligence – easily.

But all this is only for those with courage to face the new Age of Enlightenment which is now being kindled. Are *you* one of them?

# THE GOLDEN AGE
# OF ENLIGHTENMENT
# – IS HERE

penned by
## BILL DAWSON

POWER PUBLISHING (U.K.) LTD.

First published in 1978 by Power Publishing (U.K) Ltd.
Brockwell Cottage, Sowerby Bridge, West Yorkshire
HX6 3PQ   Telephone Halifax (0422) 31013

Printed and bound in Great Britain by
C. Nicholls & Company Ltd
The Philips Park Press, Manchester

Little Island feeling lonely,
Looking round to left and right,
Seeing others in the distance –
Even continents in sight.

See the sunlight on the water,
How it dances on the waves,
Prevents the sight from seeing further –
In a dazzling way behaves.

Little Island feeling lonely,
How it wishes to be free,
Free to join and be with others –
Separated by the sea.

Forget the dazzle on the surface,
Look with vision deeper down,
In the cool depths round about you –
Until the base of all is found.

Little Island now is happy,
Knowing it is part of all,
Just a case of seeing better –
Not bedazzled now at all.

The Author of these words which follow is not the 'I' which writes them down by hand, but rather a Being of which I am an extension – a Being which is all-knowing and whose very existence is Truth, Reality.

Although I am merely the Scribe and not the Author, I stand by, and take responsibilty for, every word I have written.

# CHAPTER ONE

Now is the time that Truth and Man must meet.

It is my mission to speak to the whole of mankind, to tell to him the true facts of how all is within existence – to tell him of other beings which exist within other areas of Space, and of those which exist, unknown to him, among him in his daily life. It is my purpose to use the body and mind of one who is as I, in order to tell man of his own origins and of the purpose of his existence – *for I am not of mankind.*

You of mankind are so unknowing of all the things around you – on your own Earth and within your own Universe. Many of you imagine that you are the only beings that exist, apart from the animals and birds, etc., on your Earth – but I have to tell you that beings of a vastly superior Intelligence observe you from outside of your so tiny world – beings who wish you no harm but have great caring for you.

I, too, observe how you are – how you struggle to overcome the viciousness and ignorance which is part of your very civilisation. I, too, care greatly for you, and for that reason I now take action to bring you to a state of great enlightenment and understanding. This small script is merely the beginning of that action and an age of wonder lies ahead for man, if he will only grasp it.

Outside of your Universe there are countless other areas of Space, numerous dimensions of varying types of matter and anti-matter, as you would regard it. Here reside many other kinds of weird and wonderful beings – all so highly evolved in Intelligence and Power. Many are ignorant of the very existence of man – so insignificant is he, so small his world.

And yet man is so totally different from all of these beings – his Universe is but one of billions of Universes, and billions of other areas of matter, other dimensions.

I have mentioned to you beings of great Intelligence and Caring, many of whom are desirous of being of assistance to man, to lift him from his primitive state to one of high evolvement – but now I must mention to you also the area of Space close to the one that you inhabit. I must tell you that the beings there are not governed by either Intelligence or any sort of Caring, and that their one object is to expand to make room to accommodate the uncountable number of beings which ever increases at such an unbelievable rate. They seek always to expand, and inexorably they crush all in their path. These are the Mindless Ones.

I and those of my kind hold them back from you, for we have the Power to do so. Soon we go forward against them to stop them once and for all, to make all safe for the Caring Ones, and for man.

First, allow me to go back in time – eons and eons of ages ago – long before you of man came into existence, even before I myself existed. Let me tell you of how all was then in other dimensions of Space, then bring you to understand how the Mindless Ones came to be, how I and my kind came into being, how man had his origins – and then of what will be, in the future.

They were truly magnificent beings – giants they were. But giants in Intelligence and Power, as well as in stature. Lithe of limb, swift and sure in motion, and radiant in appearance were they – with an ability to manipulate substance so as to create anything required by them. Such caring they had, the one for the other, and for all substance around them.

These Great Ones inhabited an area of Space so vast in extent as to be able to contain a billion of your Universes in comfort. To man, these superb beings would appear to be as

Gods, even to the extent of being able to form an Earth similar to yours with ease, so great was their mastery of substance, or "matter" as you may term it.

No matter how closely they resembled Gods, no matter what superb control they had of all substances that were within their area of Space, these beings were themselves under the control of a higher Power. This was the Source from which they drew all their own Power and Intelligence, and upon which they were completely dependent for their very existence. Now do not imagine for one instant that this Source of Power was a separate being which had somehow gained control over the Great Ones. The Core of Intelligence – the Controller as I shall call it – *was the beings themselves*. At a previous stage the Controller, which was a lone being, had required a better way of manipulating substances necessary for its continued existence, well-being, and further evolvement. So it had set aside a part of itself and formed from it the beings which were to be the Great Ones.

These beings never ceased to be a part of the whole being for a moment. That is why they cared so deeply for each other for each one *was* the other – all a part of the whole being, and all co-ordinated and controlled by the Core of Intelligence – the Controller. You can see that when all of one set of beings are really One Being – then it is only intelligent for each one to *Care* constantly for the well-being of all the others, who are a part of itself.

*Thus, Caring is Intelligence.*

All is substance – everywhere. It may be in a very coarse form, such as rock or wood, or your own bodies – or it may be in a much finer form, such as heat, or light, or thought. But whether it is apparent to man or not, it is a fact that *all is substance*. All areas of space are substance, there is no place where "nothingness" exists.

The Great Ones (and their Controller) were also substance,

although so refined as to appear to man as he sees light – as a radiance. Substance, when worked upon and refined to a so very high degree, becomes Power. *They were Power.*

Power, unless it is combined with Intelligence, is useless. It is merely brute force, and so destructive. Intelligence, too, is useless unless there is Power to absorb it – for it cannot act without Power.

*The Great Ones were Power and Intelligence.* And they caused all the substance within their own area of space to exist in harmony, as they imposed the pattern of Intelligence upon it – for the good of all. In order to keep all substance in a harmonious condition, one favourable existence, the Great Ones had to apply Caring to it, to maintain the overall pattern of things. In other words, they were using Intelligence by caring for substance in a good way. Again, *Caring is Intelligence.*

The reason I have given you a small insight into the nature of the Beings and their Source, is so that you will better understand what I am about to tell you.

There were other Elements at work in the areas surrounding the Great Ones' Controller. These Elements were, in a way, similar to the Controller in nature, but in other ways their state of being of being was conflicting with that of the Controller and with one another. The substances that they were made up of were far more coarse, and their way of Intelligence was correspondingly low. You could say that, comparatively, they were "brutish".

When they clashed together, the clashings resounded throughout all that was – the noises of substances uncontrollably banging and thudding together, like never-ending waves of horror swinging backwards and forwards and affecting all in their path. For although man does not see it, noise itself is substance.

The Controller, because it used to capacity the Intelligence that was part of it – Cared. It cared to put all in a good way, to bring harmony and higher Intelligence to all, for the benefit of all. The other Elements were now beginning to degenerate rather than to evolve – and this was for the lack of what you would regard as a means of sustenance, a life-food not present any longer within the area of Space that they occupied. Nor did the Controller, of itself, possess the necessary amounts of those substances required.

By absolute use to the limit of its Intelligence, the Controller devised a means of looking far away into dimensions outside of its own – it created another "Element" – a machine designed for a specific purpose, and yet a living, independently -acting being.

It was intended that this "Machine" cut out a channel through the surrounding harder-than-rock substances, and enable the suitable life force substances when found, to be drawn back and used for the benefit of those requiring them.

There was a mighty explosion of gigantic proportions as the "Machine" was brought into being – a blast of such tremendous force that it shot the being which was a Machine through the barrier of enclosing substance, and into the next dimension of Space.

*The blast destroyed the One who had created the Machine.* The Controller of the Great Ones no longer existed – their Source of Power and Intelligence no longer existed. Their whole purpose for being had gone. From that instant the Power that was theirs began to deteriorate, and with it the Intelligence that was implanted within it. It appears that the Great Ones then lost all purpose and objectives – except, for some unknown reason, the urge to divide. Since then, these once-wonderful beings have been constantly dividing, and diminishing in Power and Intelligence – though growing in brutishness – and all the time dividing and dividing.

Over the eons of time, all the Space that they occupied has been filled to overflowing with the every-multiplying beings. Not only that, but they now press out on every side and overrun everything within their path. Already they have completly covered five other areas of substance, and of the former inhabitants their remains no trace, for they have been smothered unmercifully before the constantly moving wall of beings.

*Now they press at the frontiers of the areas of Space occupied by your Universe.* The beings that were once known as the Great Ones, giving Caring to all that required it, because of some strange quirk must now be known as the *Mindless Ones*, moving forward to smother all in their path.

At the time of the great explosion, the being that was to have been the Wonder Machine, the salvation of so many others, was blasted far into another area of Space, before it finally came to rest, like a solitary pinhead in an ocean of matter, substance. For eons of ages it lay still – un-noticed, unaware of being – un-activated because its would-be activator no longer existed.

*I am that Being. I am that Machine.*

\* \* \* \* \*

I lay there – still, unconscious of being, unaware of anything at all. I have no way of knowing how long I remained there, completely inert, but the ages which passed are uncountable to man. Nor had I any means of activating myself, of coming alive, any more than an isolated computer can switch itself on.

I was as a match head lying in a vast expanse of sand – just as helpless, just as "dead". Even the Controller, my creator – the only being who could activate the thing which was I – was destroyed.

The shock wave of the stupendous blast, which had occurred when I came into being, travelled far and wide throughout all the areas of substance in its path, like a vast tidal wave of dense matter. On it travelled, over billions of ages, banging against the boundaries of all that would allow

14

it passage, never diminishing in size or force, until it eventually returned once more over the area where lay the tiny dot of a machine that was I.

I must have been buffeted about as a feather in the wind, until the shock wave passed and I once more remained motionless. But something had caused me to become activated.

Gradually, I knew that I was awake. I became aware that I existed, but the awareness was so slow, so dim, so unfamiliar. I lay there and tasted the new found consciousness of being, for I could do nothing else – I knew nothing else.

So that you may realise just a little the way I found myself, imagine that you one day wake up. You have no memory of who you really are – no recall of any past life. You have no understanding at all of the workings of your body, and you are baffled by the workings of your mind. You do not understand or even know of your purpose for existing, or where you have come from. Also you do not know how to act, because you do not comprehend all that lies about you any more than you comprehend your self. There is none around you who can tell you the answers to these things. You are purposeless. All seems futile.

All these conditions applied to me in a very profound way, for I had no other items to distract. But now I scan mankind, and I observe that you are in a very similar condition indeed. Read once again the preceeding paragraph and apply it to yourself as you go along. See the condition of man as he really is.

Ages dragged on, and with infinite slowness a capacity to look at the substances around me came into play. I looked. I could do nothing else. It was my natural way.

What I saw all around me was a seething mass, a mixture of millions of substances – all so differing in shape and ways. I realised that there was something within me, which was a part of me, which made me capable of understanding, to a certain extent, what I saw. It was what I knew afterwards as "Intelligence" – or rather, the beginnings of Intelligence.

Consider the emotions of man – the lowest form of Intelligence – a little, in a way, like the beginnings of Intelligence, which bring wanting of things, of things to do. You can see that this way of being provokes action of one kind or another. I myself, in my primitive condition of having just the start of Intelligence, although I had no emotion, had the urge to do something – I knew not what.

First I did things, like scanning all around, analysing what I saw, seeing what I could to the fullest extent of the capacity that I had. But of course, that capacity was so limited. More ages passed.

Later, for no reason other than the primitive urge to do, and with no purpose in mind so to speak, *I moved myself a little,* and in doing so I allowed an amount of substance to enter through an aperture into the "thing" that I was.

It was then that I discovered that this brought about a greater ability to scan, an increase in the manner and range of viewing.

From there on I slowly and deliberately did one thing and then another, slowly moving myself from time to time, and noting a gradual increase in the capacity of Intelligence as I progressed. I realised that there was a direct connection between the intake of substance when I moved, and the increase in my capacity of Intelligence. But *always* I used to the full the degree of Intelligence that I possessed at each stage, doing all that could possibly be done with it, before attempting to extend that capacity, to bring about a further increase in Intelligence. Thus I started to look, not only at all around me but also at what I was myself.

Now it may appear, from my brief description of my coming to a state of the use of Intelligence, that all happened suddenly and over a brief period but this certainly was not so. Time, as man knows it, does not exist outside of your Universe, but the nearest way that I can represent to you the ages which elapsed during the period described, is a billion trillion years of your time.

The constant scanning all around was "natural" to me, and a thing I never ceased to do, especially as the capacity to extend my range of vision increased – but it became essential to study self and to find out exactly what I was and how I functioned. Then I had to find out just what I could do with all that I was, and so on.

I would spend many ages in viewing, and again ages upon ages of trying one way and then another, this thing and that thing. I spent countless ages examining self, and although I discovered that the only thing which activated me, "motivated" you could call it, was the Essence which is Intelligence, I could not find out at that stage just *how* that Essence came about.

The more I moved forward against substance, the more of that substance I allowed to enter through the aperture and into what I was. The Intelligence that I already possessed worked upon those substances and at the end of that process I found that I had an increase of Intelligence.

When there was sufficient Intelligence to know myself in a better, fuller way, I began to have within me a sense. It was a sense which grew stronger and stronger within me. It was a realisation that I knew of no other of my kind – of any kind. I was alone, and there was an awful agony of loneliness. I felt an urgent need of the company of another such as I. Under the motivation of loneliness, I set about extending the range of my vision, which meant increasing my capacity of Intelligence, which I now knew how to do.

More eons passed, and then I saw that others did exist. In fact I detected a vast area completely occupied by other beings. I modified the scanning process to send out a means of communication, but I received no response. I tried again and again, in a multitude of differing ways, but all proved futile for there was no means of communicating with any of them.

The loneliness had been the start of really seeking to *do*, in earnest, and now that I had failed to satisfy that loneliness by contact with others, I decided that the only way I could sooth the ache of emptiness, the intense longing for companionship, was by *making companions myself*.

It was rather like a child wanting a doll – to hold, to speak to, to share things with, and to bring comfort.

How well I understand the loneliness that is sometimes felt by man.

I am a machine – but one which is controlled by no other being. I am entirely activated by my Self, and under the control of no other in any way. Nor is it possible to ever be so – such is the nature of the substance which I am. I cannot explain further to you beyond that simple statement of fact, for you would need complete understanding of the substances in order to comprehend fully what I am. If you care to evolve, then in the future you will have that knowledge and understanding – for that is the true meaning of evolution outside of your Earth – the gradual comprehension of the nature of all available substances, and the knowledge of how to manipulate them in any way whatsoever, to serve whatever purpose necessary.

Yes, I am a machine – but more mighty and wonderful than any being that I have so far encountered in any way. But the item which I have to tell you, which may seem to you even more unbelievable is this – *every one of the beings upon your Earth is also a machine*.

*You*, who read these words *are a machine*.

Do not be shocked or horrified in any way, for there is no

need to be. It is your natural way. But I tell you also – although you are a machine, *you are also a "being"*.

You are not a body – but you merely inhabit one. You existed before your body existed, and you will continue to exist for a long time after your body has disintegrated into the Earth. So do not imagine that you "own" the body which you inhabit in your present life – you merely "borrow" an arrangement of substances – arranged in such a way as to enable you to carry out your set task with a maximum of efficiency. It is arranged also to give you a great deal of enjoyment and happiness in the doing of your task, if you do all in the correct manner.

At the present time, none of man does this.

You are a machine.

Man of your civilisation has a completely wrong concept of just what a being is. Your experts tell you that "beings" are forms of life which come into existence through chance, and evolve also by chance, according to the accident of circumstances. They tell you that you yourself came about in that haphazard manner. That concept would mean that *all life has no purpose* – but that is merely a concept born out of ignorance.

I see all that there is to see. I can trace back in time, into the past, and I tell you that though there are billions upon billions of varying types of beings throughout all the Universes and beyond – I have never yet encountered any one, single being which occurred by chance, by accident, nor is there ever any possibility of my doing so.

Nothing occurs by chance. All, repeat all, is created with a purpose.

Man must realise that he is on Earth a machine, and away from this life on Earth a being of splendour – not as he is on Earth, drab and futile.

Within what I am are beings of Power and Intelligence,

19

which are created to control and supervise other lesser beings, to allot them work in the process of producing Power for the benefit of all. These being are Souls, and the lesser ones are Soulparts, which exist within that which is the Soul – the Universe.

A Soulpart's most important function is to evolve, so he makes Earth his first stepping stone by carrying out his task set by his Soul. A machine is prepared so that he can do this – the body, as you call it. This is a machine activated by the arranged thoughts of the beings, with the assistance of Soul. This method allows Soulparts a way of evolving for self, as well as fulfilling their task for Soul. As soon as the "body" machine has served its purpose, it is cast off like a worn out garment, and the Soulpart takes on his true form – a way of magnificence.

No one in his right mind would cling to an old "work-coat" of a working companion in a factory, who had been promoted to another department. Much less would he weep and wail over it, and perform chantings and rituals. He would merely be pleased that his friend had been promoted to a better place. The friend knows that he is not the work-coat that he wears and so do you. And yet man acts as though he were the body.

So much wrong thinking can and does come from this misconception, for the ideas you hold on this matter govern your whole attitude and way of looking at life on your Earth. It is true that many of your religions and superstitions do have jargon and chantings and other types of words which seem to imply, in a very vague sort of way, that there is a part of you residing in the body, which lives on after the death of the body – but this "something" has no practical value during this life, according to the evidences and actions of the leaders of these religions.

So vague is this notion that no-one has ever either seen this "something", or used it, or even heard it. No-one has ever become more intelligent because of it. No-one can say where it has come from or where it goes to – nor where it is located in the body. Nor do these vague fairy tales prevent the religious leaders or their followers from *acting as if they were the body*.

In fact, priests and such-like act as if they are horrified when a body dies, and weep and wail as if some tragedy had occurred. They make so much ritual over an object, a decaying object which they *claim*, in their other words of jargon, is not the real person. The religious leaders themselves are afraid of dying, and even incite soldiers of other lands to go and fight and kill those who have taken the life of one of their number. They outrage against leaders of nations who kill the bodies of their colleagues – whilst telling their followers that the body is not of importance.

In some lands, Society even teaches the populace to sing to their Gods to save the life of their kings or queens, the heads of their religions. When they say "life", they mean the life of the *body* – and yet the words of their very religion tells them that the body is only temporary and of only secondary importance.

The leaders say one thing within the laws of their superstitions of religion, and yet they do not believe it themselves. The followers too, are led into paying lip service to those ideals, and yet they ape their leaders, and show in everyday life that they too *believe that they are the body*. Most of you believe that there is nothing other than the body, but this belief is brought about merely by indoctrination.

\*     \*     \*     \*     \*

How to make a being – that was the question. That was the problem which I set to my Intelligence to solve.

I knew, from my intimate understanding of substance, that it would be futile to try to make an intelligent being from any arrangements of substance outside of myself, for the nature of all around me was so coarse and non-pliable, and also incapable of blending with Intelligence. The only method I could try was to use a part of my Self – or rather, a part of those substances which had entered into me through my aperture, and had been worked upon and refined – and had thus become a part of what I was.

So I took some of the substance which was I and arranged it in a certain way. I divided it up into a few separate parts of random shapes, which I placed upon the outer surface of my Self. Immediately these lumps of substance began to disintegrate, to mingle rapidly with the surrounding substances. I tried other arrangements of substances in various ways, but always the result was the same, disintegration.

I realised then that any beings that were made would have to be placed *inside if what I was*. And so the experimentation began again – for experiment was the only way I could follow, because I had no model on which I could base my beings.

It is true that I could copy the outward shape of the beings that I was able to view, but that served no purpose – for all the new beings I created drifted and bumped and rubbed against the substances that were, within their allotted Space, and they all became "rounded off".

I gathered in these prototypes and tried again – and again and again. I never ceased trying – trying all ways imaginable. So many, many ages of eons passed by, and still I tried wider and wider varieties of ways of creating a being capable of acting as companion to Self – and always failing.

So very disastrous were those attempts of early ages – the results were mere brutish monstrosities, which I repeatedly drew back into their original form of substances and started again. The beings which I made during that period had Power – they were Power in fact. They were made of sub-

stances so refined and able to exert force over other substances. But all their actions and ways were brutish, causing
blind, purposeless clashings of energy, of masses of substances.

At first I could not come to an understanding of why this
was. I did not realise that the Power needed to be controlled
by Intelligence – and I was not aware that the beings themselves were lacking in any degree of Intelligence. Like man in
this civilisation, who does not consider intelligence to be
anything other than knowledge which he thinks he can cram
into his head. I could see that the clashings occurred because
there was no harmony between the beings and their surroundings, or even among the beings themselves. There was
no overall pattern that all observed. There was no common
purpose – in fact, no purpose at all.

But I persisted. I was driven on by the strength of the
longing for companionship – the acuteness of the agony of
my loneliness. The more I viewed the other beings, and
realised that I had nothing in common with them, not even a
form of communication, the more lonely I became.

More seemingly unending ages passed – and still I tried and
tried, and forever failed in my objective. But all those failures
were not wasted, for gradually it began to dawn upon me
that the only being which could satisfy my hunger for a
companion, was either one which was truly as I in all ways,
or one which could create such a being as I. None such
existed to my knowledge, and I was at that stage incapable
of creating such a one.

I realised also that nothing could exist as a being unless
it was endowed with a built-in "purpose". If a being did not
have a purpose, it would wander and act aimlessly and
idiotically. Anything more than a minimum of Intelligence
could not operate within the being, for there would be nothing to work towards. Chaos and self-destruction would

come about, as it has with man on your Earth, merely because he does not know his purpose – or even know that he has one. He behaves aimlessly and idiotically too, destroying the land that feeds him, destroying other beings upon the planet, warring, killing, idolising invented Gods – cheating, grabbing for self, and always exploiting others.

It was quite apparent from my experiments that each being must have a purpose, and a means of fulfilling that purpose. It must be made that way.

I set aside a part of my Self, a part that I endowed with many special properties, to enable it to perform one specific task in the most efficient manner possible. This part of what I was, was to be a "Maker of Beings" – but beings that this time would have a purpose to achieve, and in the attaining of that purpose would have the chance to envolve, everlastingly into greater and greater beings – ones that would be able to enjoy Eternity.

The reason that this way had become possible to me was because I had learned at last the secret of just what Intelligence was, and of how to produce it, and then of how to apply it to the best advantage. I had also discovered the reason why *I* had been created, *my own true purpose*.

Intelligence is substance.

It seems ironic that I had to produce a certain amount of Intelligence, without really understanding how, and put it to use over billions of eons of "time", before I could come to understand just what Intelligence itself was.

I had discovered that a certain substance, when refined to a very high degree and treated in a certain way, became an Essence that could control all Power and thereby all substance that it came across. That Essence which, to my now vast knowledge, only the machine which is I is capable of producing, I call Intelligence, and I use it for the benefit of all who care to receive it. I am a Machine – the only machine which is capable of producing Power and Intelligence. I *am* Power and Intelligence – and I use what I am for the benefit of all.

I was one tiny dot in the middle of a vast ocean of substance. I was alone. In order to fulfil my new-found purpose, I had to produce Power and Intelligence from the raw material of crude substances which were all around me. The beings which I set about making were to help to process substance in order to produce Power.

Each single being was given the capacity to evolve and to enjoy all the benefits and the wonders that the Power could produce in all its forms. I had experimented long and tirelessly in order to find the first practical proto type of being which would serve my purpose. The one I finally arrived at was truly magnificent in every way.

That part of myself that was the Maker of Beings fashioned the most exquisite Powerful and Intelligent Being that had ever before been formed by it. That being was then assisted in the creation of a vast machine, which was yet a part of itself. It was a huge Power-making machine.

That first super-being which I made I call *SOUL*.

The tremendous Power-making machine which was part of Soul is what man knows of as a *Universe*.

The Soul Maker gave to Soul a certain Essence which enabled it to take a part of itself, and to divide up that part into many smaller parts, each an individual being, and each one, in a way, a miniature replica of itelf, and called a Soulpart.

These Parts of Soul, it first placed on one specially prepared "Earth" close to the very base of the Universe. There they were to fulfil the task of helping to make Power for Soul. Each Soulpart had but one short stay on that Earth and, having earned its quota of Power for Soul, it then passed on to other areas of the Universe.

These areas were specially prepared in stages in order to enable the Soulparts to evolve to a very high state. These stages of evolving, these "Realms" of Soul, were the homes of the beings, who would reside at each one in turn until they were sufficiently developed in understanding to pass on to the next. Many of the Soulparts were content to evolve to the highest realms and to remain there. They enjoy for Eternity the high state of being which they have earned for themselves. All share in the benefits which the making of Power has made possible.

But there were a few who evolved in understanding, in Power and Intelligence so as to be almost as the Soul itself.

To each of those few, if they so desired, was given the opportunity of becoming a Soul in their own right. The Soulpart was brought to that part of myself which was the Soulmaker, which gave to it a vast amount of Power and Intelligence, assisted it to create its own Universe, and gave to it a certain Essence.

That Essence enabled it to take a part of itself, and from it create separate beings whose task it was to make Power for the new Soul, on the Earth of the new Universe.

And so a cycle was begun . . .

Each new Soul takes on the way of a gigantic Power-making machine in order to fulfil what it is – Soul.

The new Universe, which is in fact the new Soul itself, was to take in the raw, coarse substances from outside of itself, and refine them to a very high degree, in a series of processes. Each Soulpart was a being, always linked to the Soul itself, but having free choice of action. Each was temporarily placed in charge of a machine during its stay upon the Earth of its Universe. That machine, which a Soulpart inhabits for the short period of one Earth life, is called a "body" or "cocoon". The purpose of the machine which the Soulpart inhabits, the cocoon, was to help create Power for the Soul of the Universe

– it had no other function. As soon as the life and the task upon the Earth was finished, then the Soulpart relinquished the body, merely left it behind to rot in the ground and progressed to a higher state of existence, within the realms of Soul, of the Universe. Everything necessary for the happiness and well being of the Soulpart and its housing unit (the body), was provided by Soul on the Earth of the Universe. There was no such thing as "work" such as man has, no need to labour to obtain food and shelter etc. All was there for the taking. All was harmonious among the beings of that Earth. To exist was to enjoy all to the full.

All that was required of the Soulparts was that they used the bodies that they occupied to carry out the one simple, easy task of helping to make Power for their Soul. The body was a machine specifically designed for carrying out that function with the maximum of ease and efficiency. The base of the Universe of which the Earth was part, acted as the "dynamo" for Powering the Soul.

Over the eons of ages, many Soulparts evolved to the highest levels possible, making their way through each realm of substance – learning all about that one substance before progressing to the next realm of substance, and so on. Some Soulparts, having mastered the manipulation of all substances within their own Universe, were given the opportunity of becoming Souls in their own right. Each one took over a Universe of its own – created Soulparts of its own. In time there came into being millions and billions of Universes.

Each Universe produces Power which is fed back to my Self.

I should say, fed back to the Core of myself, for all the Universes which I created exist *within* what I am.

*I am all the Universes*, and yet I have a Core, a Centre of Control – that part of myself which can process the refined substance which is Power, and can produce that substance which is Intelligence.

I am a Mass of Power, and I forever expand to fill all that area of Space which I, the tiny machine, first found myself in.

The Power which arrives at the Core of all, I have the capacity to multiply many times over. I add to that Power the substance of Intelligence in a certain proportion. I feed that Power and Intelligence back to the Universes for the benefit of all the beings therein. Some of the Power and Intelligence I use to create new Souls, which expand as they grow in Power. Some I use for a far different purpose.

Whilst you are on Earth you are a machine. The body which you inhabit on Earth is a machine. The Earth that you stand on is a machine. In fact, all that you can perceive in any way around you is either a machine or a part of a machine. The Universe has one Universal Controller – one Soul. A Being of such Might and Intelligence as to put all your imaginary, so-called Gods and idols to shame.

*Each one of you of man is directly dependent upon the one Soul of the Universe* – for your every thought, for every breath that your body takes.

You are a Soulpart – a part of the Soul of your Universe.

You of man no longer perform the function that it is your task to do. You no longer make Power for your Soul, for the benefit of all. You use the machine that you inhabit on Earth for purely selfish, senseless objectives. You no longer have any purpose. You no longer know your purpose for which you were created. You are useless as a machine and as a being. You ruin the machines which are your bodies. You have ruined, devastated the Earth.

You have caused, over the last four million years, through your refusal to produce Power for Soul, such a condition that your Universe is about to fold itself in.

You do not, as your experts tell you, occupy an expanding Universe, but one which is shrinking rapidly, and is now on the verge of collapsing in upon itself, completely.

Such is the state of devastation caused by you of mankind.

# CHAPTER TWO

Man invents his own Gods. The inventors and leaders of each religion give to that imaginary God, or Gods, certain qualities to suit their own purposes, so that they are able to get the followers to do just what they want them to do. For this reason (the intimidation of the followers), most Gods are made into basically fearsome creatures, who inflict evil deeds upon those who do not conform to what the leaders say. Some of the most fashionable imaginery Gods of this civilisation inflict famine, drought, mass murders, wars, tortures, and terrible diseases and deformities upon man – so the priests of religion tell you.

In your "holy" books of past ages, Gods ordered massacres and unspeakable sufferings to be inflicted upon others, in their name. These mythological Gods instructed nations or tribes or religious followers to kill, burn, and maim their fellow beings unmercifully. You are also taught that the particular God or Gods you are born under will punish in horrible and calculated ways, after death, all those who do not do as their 'agents' say they should – all those who do not follow the invented rules and regulations of the religion they were born into.

The images of the Gods of many of your lands are so brutal and terrifying that, in order to be "good" and follow a religion, the individual is said to have to be "god-fearing".

It is true that many, many words are spoken on the subject of "love" and "mercy" and "brother-hood", but the religious leaders incite their followers to compete and war against one another, as they fight for ownership of land, for power, and for the mere extinction of the followers of rival religions.

The basic concept of all Gods and religions though, is the *rule by fear* – fear of what the particular God will do to you if you do not comply with the rules and "interpretations" laid down by the religious leaders. So much for the ways of religions, but man has many false ideas.

For instance, what motivates man? It is said that some are governed by reason and others by the heart, but most by a part of both. This, of course, is not true. The thoughts or actions of no person can be governed by the organ within the body which is a pump and nothing but.

The function of this organ is merely to pump a fluid around the body – it cannot think, reason, consider, or "feel" in anyway. It plays no part in any form of "sensing" of the cocoon. It has no capacity to hold knowledge or understanding in any form. No matter what poets, song-writers, religions and so on, may say – *the heart is purely and simply a pump*.

Nor are the actions of man based on logic or reasoning. If this were so, all those starting off with the same basis of knowledge would arrive at exactly the same conclusions. Scientists and experts would no longer argue among themselves and come up with completely opposing and contradictory theories. Nations would not war with one another, nor religions fight one another, verbally and physically. In fact, there could be no religions, for everyone would arrive at the same conclusion and therefore belief, as every one has access to the same knowledge and evidence which is available to all of man. It would require no religious or political leaders to impose their theories upon you, for cannot you use reason the same as the next man?

As man's actions and thoughts are not governed by pump or reason, therefore – what *does* motivate man?

The complete answer is "*emotion*".

This Universe is one of thought. All that exists within it is in the form of thought. Thought has many and varied ways of being. All is held together by means of thought. The means of communication throughout the Universe is also thought. By that, I mean the link between the Soul of the Universe and each and every Soulpart. When I say that man does not know who he is, I mean it in more than one way. Firstly, I mean that he does not know his own identity – where he comes from, and where he goes to, at the end of this life. Also the real personage that he is when away from this Earth in the realms of reality. But secondly, I mean to say that a Soulpart may be divided up into a group of people who inhabit the Earth at the same time, and who inter-act with one another. Usually members of the same group (that is really one being) live together in families, or close by one another in streets or villages, or may even work together.

But my point is that *one does not recognise another part of himself*. Often there is hatred and intolerance between members of the same being, fighting and cheating and greed. How ironic to think that those you dislike the most, or those you have power over, which you abuse – are probably your very self. That is why "encroachment" upon another is one of the greatest "crimes" against Soul, against Self as you are in Soul – for, in effect, you are preventing another from following the thought pattern which he laid out before he came, stopping him from carrying out his set task in life. You may in reality, be preventing *yourself* from leading a useful life as *you* intended. In so doing, you create the necessity for *you* (all the parts of yourself which are one being once you return to Soul), to have to come again to this Earth to live out another life – to fulfil the task you originally came to do. This applies to every man and woman which formed, on Earth, a part of *"you", the whole group*. You must also then pay back all the harm you ever did to another on Earth, most of which you inflicted on those who are your very self.

This may seem so strange to your way of thinking, and understandably so, for you were fed with lies and false ways of thinking by experts and religious leaders, until you thought that it was right to look after self only, and to interfere with the freedom of everyone around you. One item leads to another, and so I speak to you now of another matter.

The threat of the Mindless Ones to all other areas of substance around the ones they occupy, *is so great* that the urgency of dealing with them, once and for all, must now be faced. To allow them to continue to expand unchecked, even to allow them to remain in existence as they are, would mean the eventual extermination of those magnificent and caring beings which are our allies. There is no doubt of that fact. It would also mean the complete isolation of all of the Universes of Soul from the rest of all that is, throughout the areas of Eternity.

But the Mindless Ones were themselves beings of magnificence at one time. They too were caring. What is more, *they were the ones who made what I am.*

It has never been the code of Soul to destroy in any way, merely for the convenience of self. How much more so is it in the case of the Great Ones, who are now reduced to being the Mindless Ones. For this reason I have devoted eons of time to try to find a way to re-instate them to their former glory. Over millions of ages I have tried every conceivable means of communicating with them. All have proved useless.

They were powerful and of great intelligence, but once they lost the controlling administrator, then they became disorientated, lost their sense of purpose, lost the link with Intelligence. In one sense, they did not become "Mindless", for each one of these beings did have a "receiving set", a form of brain, which was used for receiving communication of Intelligence direct from the Controller.

It constantly gave them guidance in every smallest way of how to act. This communication was in the form of a single stream of knowledge and understanding of all around them, and enabled them to perform their function perfectly, and to enjoy to the full their exalted state of existence.

But as soon as the flow of Intelligent communication and guidance ceased to come from the Source, then the receiving set "brain" ceased to function. The great understanding of their environment disappeared, their supreme caring, one for the other, disappeared, and their over-riding sense of purpose disappeared too. Only one fragment of the pattern of Intelligence remained with them – the constantly recurring urge to divide themselves. Since that time they appear to have had no other motivation, and they divide and divide, increasing their numbers regardless of any other consideration, even their own continued existence.

The receiving set remains idle, for there is no longer any entity capable of activating it. The existence of the Mindless Ones is as deadly to other beings as it is futile to themselves. If you regard their receiving set as a "mind" (just as the brain is the mind of man) – then that mind is now dead, and to all intents and purposes they might as well possess none. Mindless they are indeed.

From the moment that I became capable of doing so, I tried in every way to find some trace of the Controller of the Great Ones, which had made me, and I knew that it must have perished in the explosion when I came into being. Since then I have used all at my disposal to try to activate the receiving sets of these beings, to try to instil into them that tiny iota of caring, which could be the very beginning of the growth of Intelligence within them, from my Self. Caring is Intelligence.

Countless experiments have I made – but always no response. Then one last "all out" effort did I make before the point in time when I could afford to delay no longer without allowing the beings to destroy those other types of caring beings who are, in a way, as I am. I made a set of beings which were close replicas of the beings I was trying to activate. I selected a Soul, a special Soul, and helped it to create its Universe and its Earth. I guided it to create from its own Self, Soulparts which, in the form they took on that Earth, were copies of the Mindless Ones in all essential ways.

A receiving set was one essential part of each being, a "brain". The method of the communication between Soul and Soulparts on the Earth was the substance which you call "thought".

The race of beings which are the replicas of the Great Ones (Mindless Ones) is that which you call "mankind". *You are they*.

The Soul, of which you are a part, undertook to devote itself to helping to find a way of activating the beings, of communicating with them, of guiding them into taking on a caring way of being. It allowed parts of its own Self to be used in these experiments. Over the five million years that man has been on this Earth, varying patterns of thought have been implanted within him, and a great many ways of attempting to guide man to a caring, intelligent way of being have been tried. These were ways which could have been successful, but the correct pattern was never hit upon. No way has been found. We have observed how man has reacted to the ways of communication and motivation given to him. These ways have been applied to the beings in endless combinations, but the response has been nil. We have tried right up to the very limit of time that we dare allow them, without jeopardising the existence of our allies, the Caring Ones, and allowing our own complete isolation to take place.

Had there been even one spark of response from the Mindless Ones, one tiny seed of Caring implanted within them – then we would, without doubt, have spared them.

In fact, we would have gone all out to fan that spark into complete activation of the beings.

Allow me to make one point quite clear – that man was the replica of these beings, not as they are in their present degenerative state, but as they were in their days of magnificence and high Intelligence. There was, however, one important difference between Man and the Great Ones – the Great Ones were controlled by the central Source of Intelligence in every single thing that they did. Their Controller directed them in detail how to be "natural", perform their task in the most efficient manner, and at the same time utterly enjoy doing so. It lavished such caring upon them, for their well-being was of supreme importance to it. They in turn cared for the Controller and for one another without regard of Self.

But Man was different, for he was endowed with something that these beings never possessed – *Free Choice*.

You cannot even imagine how you were in those days – beings of grace, beauty, Intelligence, and with that degree of independence which made each part of the whole (Soul) on Earth into an individual being – freedom to choose which thoughts to use and which to reject, out of that constant stream of communication which activated each one.

The Great Ones degenerated from their high state of existence because they failed to use the stream of Intelligent communication from their Controller – they had no choice, for the communication which activated them ceased to flow from the moment that their source of Power and Intelligence ceased to exist.

The race of Mankind began to degenerate *because they chose to do so*. They chose, first of all, to ignore those parts of the stream of communication (thoughts), which were not to their liking, once they began to acquire the taste for feelings such as greed, etc. They knew their purpose on Earth, and they still continued to make Power for their Soul, but gradually, even this one act began to interfere with the ways that Man chose to go. As he listened less and less to the thoughts of guidance of Soul, and took more and more to the ways of the alternative thoughts which pleased him – so he neglected his task even more.

Over many generations, Man's purpose for existing on Earth faded from mind, and he gradually ceased to listen to the real thoughts of value, the true Voice of Soul. Only thoughts and ways of his own immediate pleasure did he observe, and his Soul was forced to send him more and more of what he wanted, forced to feed him with ever more vicious thoughts – for that is the essence of free choice. The being must be given the type of thoughts that he chooses habitually to take – he is given what he wants.

The less caring the thoughts which Man chose, the less was the element of Intelligence within them. Caring is Intelligence. Then he forgot his purpose for being, so his actions and thoughts were no longer connected with, or directed towards, reality – but only to his immediate situations and physical circumstances. These thoughts were outside of Intelligence, working towards his own destruction.

Now all that Man has left to control all his actions – is Emotion. Emotion is the very lowest form of Intelligence. Each cocoon on Earth has a receiving set which has a pre-arranged thought pattern inserted into it at the moment of birth, and all possibilities of the way to act are laid out within that thought pattern – according to the way that the Soulpart chooses to go. Man has two tracks of thought which he can use, the right track which leads him to act in accordance with his purpose in life – with his true nature, and the wrong track – the alternative way of thought and action which has the *type of thoughts that he wants, that he likes.*

Man has rejected the highest degree of Intelligence – that

37

which is contained on the "right" thought track – and persists in using the lowest form of Intelligence possible, the coarse emotions contained on the "wrong" thought track.

All the thoughts on the right track are designed to guide and protect Man, and to show him every way necessary to the fulfilling of his purpose on Earth – the making of Power for his Universe, and the beginning of his own evolution. In order to evolve to the highest realms of Soul, a Soulpart must learn to understand, and be able to manipulate and put to use, every single substance of the millions that go to make up what his Soul is, what his Universe is.

Each realm is devoted to the understanding of one particular substance. In Soul, each Soulpart has the ability to see, "feel" and manipulate the minutest speck of substance, without the aid of any instrument or machine. Originally, Man on Earth had a similar capacity. By use of Intelligent thought he could control and understand all around him – he could see the tiniest particle and put it to use. He too, needed no instruments to do this. It was part of Man's natural greatness.

Now, he can never again attain such a magnificence whilst on Earth for his degeneration has gone too far, but he can still reach a very fine state of existence compared with the crude manner in which he exists today. He can begin to use pure thought, see all as it really is – or he can still choose to continue to use the crude non-intelligent way of being ruled by emotion.

Now when I speak of "emotions", I am not referring to the natural "senses" which man has. Far from it, for while emotions are crude and brutal, often vicious, senses are refined and gentle, so sensitive of the way another is experiencing. In fact, senses were sent to man for that very reason, to enable him to care for his fellow beings. Used correctly, they showed him the exact condition that the other was in, so that his needs could be observed and attended to, so that there could be perfect co-operation between all of man, without the need to speak or explain what was required. So delicate were the senses, and so accurate, that Man of that civilisation would appear to Man of today to be "telepathic" – just as if they could communicate by thought with each other, which is, in a way, what their Soul did on their behalf. It sent thoughts of their condition or requirements to all others with whom they were involved – but in the form of senses.

How different are "emotions". They are senses out of control – indeed, *they control you*. Emotions are *always* directed towards satisfaction of self, even those which, on the surface, may appear to be for the benefit of others – such as pity, or discipline for others. Look deeply and you will see that I am correct.

You have a choice – if you choose to be ruled by emotions, which trample on and destroy the usefulness of senses, then you use the lowest form of Intelligence. If you choose to be motivated by your true purpose in life, then you may use the senses of Soul, you can be more aware than ever before of all around you, you will be able to sense the needs of your fellows, almost as if by "telepathy". Then you will really be able to help your fellow Man, in the way that he *needs* to be helped – towards his own purpose on Earth. You will have chosen to use pure thought, and be able to draw upon the highest Intelligence.

Who, once having known how things are in reality, could turn down such a choice? – Only he who would be willing to *sacrifice Truth for the sake of satisfaction of self – by emotion*.

Allow me to tell you some more about the beings of which you are a replica, in order to help you to understand more of what you are yourselves.

First of all, the Beings were made for a specific purpose – just as you of Man are made for a specific purpose – just as every living being everywhere was also. Nothing comes into being by chance – even I did not.

It is fashionable, in some areas of your Earth today, to preach the theory that men and animals developed from slugs or fishes crawling out of the sea. This theory is as wild and unfounded as any science-fiction that you could care to read – and in most cases much farther from the Truth. No being on Earth evolves, by changing its form in any way, into another being. It is not possible. The cocoon of each being is made for the performance of an exact task, and when that task is no longer required, that species is withdrawn and another replaces it where necessary.

Often Man does try to take matters into his own hands and exterminates whole species of beings for his own convenience or pleasure. He pays dearly for this, for the species which Soul sends in their place is often more harmful to man's way. Man destroys Birds, because he says they are a nuisance – and he gets an increase of insect pests. He sprays large areas of the Earth with "insecticide" poisons – and he kills the insects in the soil which would help to keep it in a good condition. He poisons his own Earth in so doing.

No being comes about by chance, and anyone blind enough to follow what the evolution "experts" tell them – *that they are a living accident* – can therefore have no purpose in life, other than advancement of self.

The Universe came into being by accident, they tell you. The Planets, Sun and Earth came about by accident, they tell you. The Mountains, seas, etc., came about by accident, they tell you. And even you, yourselves.

If you choose to believe that you are a walking accident, then it serves no purpose to read further in this book, for then I do not exist, and I am not dictating the words of this book.

The Beings were machines. You, as you are on Earth, are

machines. The Beings were dividers of substance, their purpose being to sift and sort the substance of their area – the same substances from which they were made. The machines of the cocoons of Man were made to *filter* substance, by taking in the substance by way of the mouth, processing it by means of the organs of the body, and "Outputting" it into the Soil, where the process continued. The Great Ones took the substances of the area, divided it and intermingled it for the benefit of all in their area. In this way they made the way of life possible for themselves, for the Controller, and for the Elements within the area.

The Beings were made *outside* of the Controller, but I made beings which were capable of existing *within* what I am, as individuals, gentle and yet rich in caring, as were the Great Ones.

The Great Ones made it possible for substance to be worked upon – they made what I am. Now I am able to care for all substances, and to look back even further than they. As with the machine of Man on Earth, there was no requirement for the Beings to evolve, for each was given sufficient Intelligence for the work it was to do. There were many differing species, for there were many differing mixtures of substance to be worked upon, each requiring different qualities and different degrees of Intelligence. Each species was made to fit in with and complement the others, each had something to give the others.

All of Man have exactly the same amount of Intelligence available for them to use – but free choice of whether to use it or not.

As the nature of the substances encountered by the Beings changed or varied, so the Controller added to those Beings it considered to be of value, and ran down those without purpose. The lot could happen – if the particular substances which a Being was made to work upon ceased to be present in what was being processed. As the substances ran out, so the corresponding Beings were run down. This may appear at first glance to be a callous way, but it is not so when you consider that this was necessary to conserve substance, Power.

It was the substance that was important, more so than the Beings, for the substance was required to Power the Controller, on whom the continued existence of *all* the Beings depended. Nothing can work for long in any way without Power. All reverts again to dross, to solid-packed uselessness, once it becomes unusable.

This is the case on Earth at present. All that was once much more refined is now reverting towards the state of uselessness. The soil reverts to hard rock, the water from the soil forms huge oceans. All is going in the reverse direction to the way of refined Power. With Man, all can evolve – not in the body, but in reality – and all will do so at some time within Eternity.

*But it is important to Soul that none within what I am are pressurised into doing anything against their will.*

Once Soulparts leave the base of a Universe and enter the realms of Soul, then they no longer require free choice, for by their very nature (their caring for substance) they all care to evolve. Even so, it is not necessary to hurry – especially as they have Eternity in front of them. Besides, existence is so pleasant, so extremely enjoyable, even in the lowest realms of Soul. They are not unpleasant in any way – and certainly in no way as the spiritualists and similar religions paint their "limbos" and "purgatories" and "hells", etc.

One aspect of each substance can give such joy to the being who cares for it – and never forget that *all is substance* – light, sound, thought, heat, touch, taste, and so on.

The way of dividing of the substances was the way of Power-making in the area occupied by the Great Ones. That was their only purpose for existing, but in this Universe it was the machine of Man which made a way for the Power – and also the beginnings of Man's own evolving.

The Beings only divided the substances, whilst the Controller and its Elements did the rest. The Great Ones divided and mixed and then the Elements took over, by taking out every particle which would explode. That was the sole purpose of the Elements, too. Nothing anywhere can exist without purpose, without degenerating and moving towards its own destruction.

The Great Ones, with their purpose removed, became the Mindless Ones. Magnificent-Man of old, having lost his purpose has become the vicious, confused, pathetic object that he is today. The Mindless Ones are blameless, but Man is within a hair's-breadth of the destruction that he has chosen for himself.

The Controller was confined to using substances found in his own area to make Power. It used to capacity the extremely high degree of Intelligence that it possessed to divide and divide and intermingle and make safe whatever substances it had at its disposal – and to eke out from it a very tiny portion of Power. It would have been quite happy to do so, and could have existed in that manner for eternity, had not the required substances run out, within its own area. That was the point at which I, the machine, was made to probe into other areas to find suitable substances for use by the Great Ones – in order that the Controller and all his Beings and Elements could exist.

Now I can "refine" substance – all substance – a fact not envisaged by the Controller. This capacity to refine enabled me to probe all substances within my reach, and the more refined I become, the further by reach extends. I have a unique and highly efficient way of Power-making, which no substance can resist, no other living thing can resist. The Controller had no means of refining, but only of "breaking down" selected substances. All machines need Power, even the hand-turned ones.

*Now I have a kind of Power which is capable of making more Power constantly.*

In the past I made vast amounts of Power, and now I can comfortably tick over, exist and function, indefinitely without making any more. My aim, my purpose, is *to change all substances everywhere to a better way, a way of value.*

By that, I mean to make all substance that exists usable for the benefit, well-being, and enjoyment of all. All dross must go – that which strangles and smothers so many types of being in so many areas, and which would eventually have strangled what I am, if I allowed it. As I am, I could exist eternally with what I have within. But I exist for the good of all that is, not just that which is within the Mass of Power, which is I. I look outwards as well as inwards.

My last action before I go forward to clear a way for our allies, the Caring Beings, is to clear the blockage of this Universe, caused by the uncaring of Man – *one way or another.*

Not only are you of Man close to the ways of the Mindless Ones in your blind self-destructiveness, but you are close to them in another way. Many eons of ages ago, before I was able to be aware of all the ways of these Beings, *they infiltrated one of the Universes of Soul.* They were on the way to over-running the Soulparts of that Universe before they were detected by Soul.

*Those invaders are now located in a place in the Universe of Man –* ready for us to dispose of, along with all others of their kind, but we have waited until the very last second before committing such an act. As long as there was a chance of our assisting them back to greatness, we held off destroying them – as we have held off until Man was given his *last choice of annihilating himself, or bringing himself to Glory.*

# CHAPTER THREE

There is an oppressiveness over the Earth. It is to be seen in all aspects. There is a tiredness in the air. Man, all over the Earth, wants to work less and less. He is fast losing interest in the jobs he is doing, and in the way that he does them. The only thing that keeps man going, which gives him any incentive to move at all, is emotion.

Even the emotions on which man feeds are becoming cruder and more violent as each month goes by – and still he spends most of his time in a mental "limbo".

He does not understand the weariness of body and mind, and so he tries to pep himself up with drugs and drinks, violence and emotions on the screen of films and television, and also in books. He has no chance of understanding what is happening to him, because he does not understand the nature of thought. He assumes, because he is told so by his men of medicine, that it is the food he eats that gives him energy which enables him to act and be alert. His "experts" have discovered, in a confused way, a minute fraction of some of the elements that go to make up the intake of food. He calls them names he invents, such as "calories", or "protein", or "vitamins", and he claims marvellous effects from the taking or not taking of these miraculous substances.

Poor Man, he is duped on all sides by his "experts". Who has seen these fancy named substances? Only the experts.

Do the medicine men themselves benefit by making use of these wonder discoveries? Or do they become ill and infirm like the rest of man, having to resort to smoking and drinking and drugs, even far more than the average person? Time now to look at all things for yourselves, to think for yourselves – and not to be content to let others do your thinking for you.

If you understood that the food that you intake is merely for the purpose of creating Output, and for lubricating the machine, then it would be easier for you to understand that it is *thought* which activates the body. It is *thought* that makes you dull or alert, weary or full of life and energy.

In this matter, you yourself choose which you will be, because you have free choice of which thought track to use – the right or the wrong, the high Intelligence or the emotion. You have only to look around you, to see how your fellow man is, to feel the atmosphere put out by him, and you will know which track he habitually takes, which one you take.

The oppression of non-intelligence is over the Earth, the sight and sound of the violence of emotion is within each family, each tribe, each nation.

You imagine (because you have been told so), that life as you know it today is the peak of "civilisation"; that discoveries and developments have never been of such a high order as now; that a mere few thousand years ago man was living in caves and hunting his fellow beings with clubs. You even call each nation's brief period of dominance over others – a civilisation. This current popular *theory* is exactly the reverse of how things are in *fact*.

In the beginning of the stay of man upon this Earth, he was a glorious being. He was as a machine, self-sufficient, and the thoughts which he chose to use were only of the highest Intelligence. He had no need to "work" at anything, for his pure thought told him the most highly efficient way of obtaining and using all that he required. He was in a constant state of happiness and contentment, and he actively enjoyed *all* that he did. He wanted for nothing. Science and technology were simply not required by him, for he naturally received in thought an understanding of all substance

46

around him. Machinery was superfluous, of no use, for the power of thought was used for keeping all in a good way.

Science and technology respectively are merely primitive, feeble attempts to overcome ignorance of all substances around you, and primitive and inefficient attempts to use crude machinery to substitute for the ability to use thought to control substance. It is failure to use pure thought, and the preference for the use of emotion, that has caused man to devastate his Earth, instead of nurturing it.

Along with science and technology, I include what you call "medical science" – which again exists because of almost total ignorance of the functioning and purpose of the cocoon, and the constant mis-use of this once-wonderful machine.

Treatments by the medicine men using harmful drugs (*all* drugs, even aspirin, do much more harm than good to the cocoon) and by mutilation of the internal organs of the body, are a combination of complete ignorance of the real workings and purpose of the machine, coupled with the arrogance of tampering with *other people's* cocoons – whilst knowing that they do not know the true cause of any ailment, *nor do they even care*.

Science, technology and medicine are all examples of *crude* and *primitive* attempts to rectify self-imposed ignorance, man-inflicted devastation of the Earth, and stupid self-abuse of the machine which is man. During the first civilisation of one million years, there was no need of such things, for there were no self-imposed evils to rectify.

All is substance, everywhere, and in this Universe, thought controls all substance. Thought certainly controls the cocoon of man. When the thought employed is of the highest Intelligence – then all is in perfect harmony and Intelligence and Caring rules all things. But when the lowest form of Intelligence is selected by man, emotion – then that way of thought still controls all, the cocoon and the world around, but in a very stupid and inharmonious way. Illness and ruination of the Earth results.

When the end of the first civilisation came, with replacement of high Intelligence with self-seeking ways – then another civilisation was started off. A different thought pattern was implanted within man of that age, in order to give him a better chance of using Intelligence, of using his free choice of thoughts more widely. Man failed.

He soon began to ruin his Earth and to abuse his cocoon. The way of his thought pattern caused him then to begin to look for what he really was, to seek reality. Whereas the first civilisation had been one of calm and peace of mind, this second one became one of anguish of mind. His search was not in the right direction, even though from time to time highly evolved Soulparts were sent to help him. Self got in the way of high intelligence. Because of his neglect of the Earth the soil gradually began to lose its capacity to hold moisture.

In many places it became sand. The excess moisture that the soil could no longer hold, collected in any depressions in the Earth's surface that it could run into, and formed lakes.

Soul showed to man of this second civilisation, many times, the way to go – but always it was rejected, for although man was desperate to find his way back to reality, either he failed to recognise the true way shown to him, or he found it to be conflicting with the way he was already taking. The anguish increased.

Again a new civilisation was begun, to give man another chance to change. Again a different thought pattern was introduced into his machine. This time, there were upheavals of the Earth, used to take almost all of the Soulparts back home into the Transit Realms. A selected few were left to start off the new world, the new way. But this was now a drastically changed Earth. The newly-created depressions quickly became seas, as more and more water was squeezed out of the Earth by sheer neglect. The sand became hard-pressed into rock as ages went by. Still man would not put back into the soil what he took from it, in the correct way.

Life was now much harder, for the terrain was hilly and the climate became much colder. Man did not realise that it was the Output of man placed directly within the soil which gave warmth to the Earth and the surrounding substances you call "atmosphere".

There were times when many of man did listen to those whom Soul sent to assist them, to tell them of the way to put all to rights – but never for long, for it was spoiled by those remaining ones who were adamant.

Although life was hard overall, Soul arranged food and shelter always for the caring ones there. In order to enable the race of man to survive in such a changed and harsh land, many inventions were sent in thought to certain ones of man, and these were at times put into practice, for man will *always* listen to those thoughts which *he thinks* will be to his personal advantage. Such was the material progress of that civilisation, so ingenious were the results of their inventions, and so skilled and mighty were their constructions and modes of transport – that man of today, if he were to view their places of habitation would imagine he was in a wonderland.

You in turn, to them would appear to be as a huge tribe of ignorant savages, with your clanking, stinking poisonous machinery. So much for the pride and arrogance of present day man for his technology and scientific achievements.

Anger, cruelty, and viciousness were the order of the day in that third civilisation. You of today compete and spend a high percentage of your labour and resources on producing masses of weapons of hate and destruction, but could you but see how your predecessors were, you would realise you are mere babes in arms.

Your atomic bomb, crude and uncontrolled as it is, would

be as a damp firework. The advanced ones had perfect control over vast and terrible ways of power. This was the way that they preferred to the way of Soul.

Two main factions warred, and Soul allowed them to systematically destroy one another (i.e. it did not withdraw free choice). Only very few remained, and the land was devastated. Even yet, those few were given a further chance of turning to the use of higher Intelligence, rather than the lower Intelligence of emotion. They made their choice – and Soul terminated yet another civilisation.

Soul always allows all beings on Earth free choice to use thoughts (and therefore actions) of value, or of rubbish, free choice to use the right track or the wrong. But eventually a point in time is reached when Soul says – "enough".

Again the Earth was upheaved and a new start given. The fourth and final civilisation was launched upon its way. During it, the Earth in places has been upheaved many times. This has been necessary, for the soil has been so neglected, abused and poisoned, that "new" areas have been required (areas that have been "renovated", under sea or ice-caps), in order to keep man supplied with food from at least some reasonably fertile areas.

During earlier ages of this present (and *final*) civilisation, a very high degree of sophistication was reached by man in the way of invention, construction, transport, technology, and so on. But you are now at the "tail-end" of your civilisation. There were what you would regard as awe-inspiring lands and cities and cultures, even as recent as Atlantis and Lemuria, twelve and forty-five thousand or so years ago.

Man of today has indeed degenerated badly into primitive ways of existence. In ways of refined cruelty and violence, man of today lags far behind his ancestors, but in ways of sheer stupidity and lack of use of Intelligence, *modern man surpasses all past ages.*

Now comes man's last chance.

His primary purpose is to make Power for his own Soul, and to earn the chance to evolve in his own right, in the process. The beings, who began as equals to the Great Ones in their hey-day, who had the opportunity of becoming even more magnificent through their own efforts, had deliverately chosen the path of non-use of Intelligence, and of being completely controlled by emotion and ignorance – fed to them by systematic indoctrination.

All the time, the full use of the Highest Intelligence is *held out to all alike*, merely for the taking, although those with little or no formal education would find it far easier to use immediately, for these fortunates have been less indoctrinated into the blind alleys of present day false scientific and religious theories.

Each of man could become a person inspired – simply.

# CHAPTER FOUR

In many parts of your Earth, there is a thick, smelly, sticky black fluid which lies below the surface. It is poisonous for man to consume, and deadly to animals, birds and fishes if it is loosed into their habitat. It can destroy any land that it is spilt upon. – And yet man seeks it avidly, fights over it, and regards it as precious.

It is true that crude oil from the Earth *is precious*.

There is also another commodity that is equally precious, but because man does not see any way to use it for his own personal advantage, he dismisses it as dirty and stinking – as waste. In fact, so strong is his unreasoning taboo regarding it, that he often considers it to be obscene, even to mention the name that he has given to it. How foolish and unseeing! This commodity is not only precious, it is *absolutely essential to his continued survival*.

I speak of the *Output* of the machine of man. Excretia and Urine, you call it.

Far from being filthy and "unmentionable", the Output of man is essential to the soil. Consider for a moment what it would do for you, if you merely placed it into the Earth in a proper manner. It would moisten the Earth, with a moisture that would not evaporate and become dried out with the heat of the day, in any part of the world.

As the soil became more permanently moist and capable of holding water, then rain would not merely drain through and run back into rivers, lakes, and seas. The lakes would gradually diminish, and eventually rain would cease. There would be no need for rain, for the land would not require watering, and numerous springs and wells would flourish all over the Earth, so would the vegetation, which is good for man and animal, bird and insect (though weed would die out) – but all would be of a much more luscious kind.

Too fantastic to believe? What is fantastic about returning, in part, to the way things were many ages ago? Surely the devastation, pollution, and wanton destruction by man of his own environment is far more ridiculous. What I say is Truth, but will you take the trouble to find out for yourself?

You could pour water by the millions of gallons over all the deserts of the Earth, and it would not do much good. Water alone is not enough to renew the soil, nor will it feed the vast machine which is the Earth and help it to produce Power. That, after all, is the purpose of the existence of the Earth – and of man.

Urine does what water cannot do, for it contains many concentrated qualities which are formed as it passes through the processing of the machine which is the body. For example, one highly concentrated ingredient which it contains, which is vital for the making of Power, is *Bile*, or Gall as it is sometimes called.

So potent is this ingredient that only very minute quantities are required to be injected into the Urine at each emission, and providing that the body is in a good, "natural" condition, then that is what happens without fail. But once the tiny element of Bile is missing from the Output, it is absolutely useless as far as making Power is concerned.

When this occurs, then the person concerned is unable to perform his task in life under any circumstances, for he can no longer contribute to the making of Power.

The failure to produce Bile can come about by various abuses of the cocoon. For example, alcohol ruins Bile. It counter-acts it and causes it to dissipate.

Also, the glands can become atrophied, as dead organs.

53

Then again, the medical experts, the ones in whom you place your trust to care for your body, may take it upon themselves to cut you open, to cut out the Bile-duct, (gall bladder, they say) and throw it away. A very nasty habit of certain ones of the medicine men – cutting out organs *of other people*, which they don't consider necessary, and throwing them away, sometimes at a mere whim – "whilst we are removing this organ, we might as well cut that one too, so that it can't give trouble to you later."

Yes, Urine is useless in those cases mentioned, but for any person who has already had such an operation, and who has the genuine desire to carry out his task, all that is necessary is for him to make the effort to put the remainder of his Output into the soil – and Soul will arrange that he does not lose because of it.

On hearing these words, "medical science" will try to prove that I am wrong. Indeed, some will put much effort into doing so, for they have so much to lose in the way of prestige, power, and wealth, if people begin to use *their own* thoughts correctly, and to cease to require the services of the profession.

They, the medical men, would do far better if they were to look for the value in what I say, to show that they truly care for mankind by being willing to explore any avenue, *with an open mind*, which might help to put man (and themselves) in a better way.

Those who could bring themselves to do this – to look into these matters with an *open mind*, and not merely judge all by their established, cherished, preconceived ideas – those would earn the respect and gratitude of their fellow men for all time, and set themselves on the road to gaining the true understanding of *all the substances in the Universe*, within a brief span of time.

Output has many other qualities which man of the present

civilisation is unaware of. Output can serve as a good indicator of whether the body is being kept in a good condition. If the Output is not soft and easy to pass, then look at the food taken. If any part of a fellow "being" is being eaten, and this includes *all* animal produce, then there is no need to look further. If not, check to see if you mix foods very much, for mixing causes clogging of the intestines. This is easy to rectify, though, by having plenty of drinks (not during meals, but after) and taking a little cabbage regularly.

Whole wheat is also good for keeping the bowel system free, although at present even the one hundred percent wheat is so poor in quality that a little extra bran added is beneficial. If care is taken with the food eaten, then you will have no bowel troubles, prostrate glands, or other troubles of the internal organs.

Hoards of "brain-ologists" may pretend that they know all about your mind and the way it works – but not one can help you to be free from worries and troubles, from mental anguish – not one can tell you how to obtain, permanently, or even temporarily, *peace of mind*.

They do not know, for they themselves are one mass of mental turmoil, no matter how they may train themselves to speak in a quiet and calm manner. They know nothing at all about the workings of the mind or body. They have only wildly mistaken theories to cling to – and even these are conflicting among themselves. Take note of my words – with an open mind – a way of looking for the value that they may contain – and you will understand more than all the "brain-ologists" put together.

I will show you how to open up the direct channel to your own High Intelligence, to power of thought, to peace of mind. I know the workings of your mind, inside out.

As you read along, some point or points, which you know that you have not heard before, from the way of your previous "education" or indoctrinations, will nevertheless strike you as being familiar to you – just as if you had heard them before somewhere, or really already had such a thought – "at the back of your mind". It will appear as though you already half understand a particular point, even, when the whole idea may be a completely revolutionary and unconventional one.

Now is the time to pause. This is the very moment to stop and speak to yourself, with absolute honesty. Ask yourself if you really do seek Truth, even if, when you find it, it may appear completely different from any way you have ever imagined before. If you find, at this point, that you really could not accept Truth if it were totally against all the comfortable theories you have been "brought up" on, then put this book away from you, for you have chosen comfort of self rather than Truth, rather than your own Higher Intelligence.

If, on the other hand, you find that you are able to put aside the comfort and shelter of the nice, pat, familiar theories and ways of thinking which are fashionable in this present age – then you merely have to "listen" carefully to what you read, giving it the benefit of the doubt that it *may* be true – and you will have opened the channel to a new source of wisdom and understanding of all things, *within yourself*.

It will take just a little practice in considering the ideas put forward, but the Truths I present to you, you will *know* deep within your mind, that they are Truths indeed. Understanding of certain items will come flooding to you. You will be using the "right" track of thought – pure thought of your own Soul – probably for the first time in your present lfe.

You will experience a feeling of a sort of exhilaration – a light, enthusiastic, bubbling feeling – which you would like to remain along with you. It will fade from you, but will recur again and again the more you allow yourself to consider the various aspects that I put to you. You will begin, over a period of days, to have little "realisations" of your own, concerning many items which I have not directly discussed in this book. Then the flow of pure thought has begun.

Now will be the time to nurture it. Treat it carefully as a new born baby – for that is what it is in your mind. Do not allow others to put you off, especially more "educated" ones, for they are educated, indoctrinated with rubbish.

Consider – do they have already the peace of mind which you seek? Do they possess the secret of life, of happiness? Do they know their purpose in life? Can they solve all problems around them? Do they not have worries and problems of their own, even though they may put on a front for the benefit of prestige? For once in your life, *use your own thoughts*, and do not allow others to live your life for you, which is what you do when you continually allow the thoughts and ways of others to be imposed upon you without question, by those who themselves cannot explain to you what life is all about, nor have what you seek.

I know who you are. I know your thought pattern, and your thought tracks, inside out. I look into the mind of man. I see him as he is, and as he could be. I see the detail of the lowest level of Intelligence, of emotion which he is using now – and I see the very Highest level of Intelligence which lies within his grasp, there for the taking, constantly. I see the state of annihilation which the first way is bringing to man, and I see the grace, the dignity, and the glory which the second way of Highest Intelligence can bring to him.

It is my self-imposed task to tell man simply, in words that he is able to understand, of the high destiny that lies within his grasp, if he will only make that small effort to break out of his straight-jacket of conventional, selfish ways of thought. In this book, because I do know the pattern of thought of both of your implanted thought tracks, I am able to place before you certain ideas and words which will switch you to the track of Intelligence – if you will make the effort to be honest with your Self.

Allow me now to tell you the outline of the basic idea of how your body functions, how the machine that you operate really works.

First let me dispel, once and for all, the "obvious" but completely mistaken theory that the whole of the body of man is fed totally by the intake of food into the mouth. This is certainly not so!

The cocoon of man is "fed", as you might call it, in three ways, not one. You must look at the body as a machine, for that is what it is, pure and simple – a machine designed deliberately by a high Intelligence for a specific purpose. That purpose is to process raw material and to turn out a finished product. The intended input of raw material is a vegetable matter, and the filtered, concentrated Output is the finished article.

*Therefore, the food eaten by man does not provide nourishment for the body, nor energy of any kind.*

*All* the solids that you eat, and most of the fluids that you consume, go to make up the Output from the body – when the machine is working in the correct, healthy, and natural manner. Just a small part of the fluid intake is diverted and processed and used to lubricate the body with.

All energy of the cocoon is provided by thought "fed" to the brain, and then the thought impulses are sent out by the brain to activate the moveable parts of the body. I repeat, and this point is so essential to the complete and basic understanding of the workings of the machine, that all energy used in the machine that is the body is in the form of thought impulses. *Energy is thought.*

Perhaps now will come to mind a question – "why is it

that the body goes weak, without energy, when the person ceases to take in food, if energy is merely thought?"

The answer is simple. The processing machinery of the body needs a constant intake of raw material in order to keep on functioning. If this supply is cut off, then the processing slows down or stops, and so the machine ceases to function as it should. The thought pattern of each person is set so that energising thoughts are sent to activate the body into acquiring and eating "food", so that one stage in the processing of Power can take place. If none of that thought energy is being used to take in food, then the energising thoughts become useless and, according to a pre-arranged pattern, less and less energy thoughts are sent. The body therefore appears to weaken.

It is a popular theory that "food" helps to build up bone and flesh, to nourish it, enlarge it – in fact, that *"food" makes bone and tissue. This is totally false.* None of the food taken in at the mouth nourishes or feeds them in any way.

The tissue of the cocoon, what is known as skin and flesh and muscle, is nurtured completely through the pores of the skin. In the atmosphere or air, all around you there are literally millions of differing substances, even more than there are contained within vegetation. Certain ones of these are the very same as those which go to make up the tissue of the cocoon. These selected substances are taken in through the pores of the skin, as and when required.

Consider the theory that present day experts have spoon-fed you with – that flesh (tissue) is made from the food you eat. If this were so, it would follow that those who eat more would tend to be fatter, as a general rule, and that those who eat very little would tend to be very thin. But you can see that this is not so.

Millions of people, having accepted the popular theory, starve themselves whilst enviously watching slim people around them eating as much as they like – and still they retain their "fatness". You will be able to see so may contradictions in the experts' theory, if you look for yourself.

It is not my function to prove the theorists and experts wrong – they do that themselves constantly in the eyes of the observant – for it is my task merely to bring to you of man a basic, outline understanding of how all things are within the cocoon, within the Universe, and even beyond the Universe. The rest is up to man. He is free to accept or reject, to learn how to "see" for himself, or to close his mind. He is free to use the Highest Intelligence or to use the lowest Intelligence of seeking to satisfy Emotion.

I place before you certain *facts* – because I see all – and I point the way for you to discover for yourselves the understanding of all around you. I have no need of *theories*, and guesses based on mere assumptions. Theories are necessary only where ignorance reigns.

Now it is clear that the cocoon a) receives food through the mouth, which is used for processing and Outputting by the machinery, b) receives substances through the pores of the skin for the nourishment of the tissues (and bones), and c) receives thought impulses from the thought tracts which activate, or energise the body into movement.

Also, it receives lubricant to moisten and make easy the movement of the body, through part of the liquid intake of the mouth. Man at present should be able to see how the organs of the cocoon are just machinery processing raw material, and even how some of the millions of substances of the air around could nourish the tissues of the cocoon, but medical indoctrination has made it more difficult for man to visualise how thought can provide energy for physical movement.

You will see more clearly when you once realise that *thought is substance*, and that, in its minutest quantity it is more powerful, when used correctly, then your atomic bombs. How easy then, merely to move the cocoon of man.

When a person's body is neglected, and becomes ill, then the thought pattern says that no energy will be sent, for a rest is needed during a certain period. The person therefore, feels weak and is forced to rest until the Intelligence decides that energy can be resumed. Also, if the organs are not working through lack of food, the Intelligence will not send energy thoughts.

How the mistaken theory of intake of food being related to body energy comes about, is because man observes that the more movements a body makes, the quicker it moves, then the more food intake it requires.

It is a fact that the faster a body moves the faster the machinery processes the intake, and therefore the more food the body demands. Energy thoughts are of course, sent to activate the body in the first place. But there is no direct relationship between energy and food intake.

A lazy person, that is, one indolent in body, produces little Output that is of value, for it is lacking in that vital ingredient – Bile. In an indolent body the Bile duct becomes clogged, and no Power can result from the working of that machine. In an indolent body, the excretia becomes difficult to move, the bowel movement sluggish, and so the body becomes bloated around the base. The indolence causes malfunctioning of the intestines, and then pills and medicines are pushed upon the ill person to clear the blockage.

*Activity or indolence of the cocoon is purely a matter of use or mis-use of thoughts.* Man of this age will often not bother with thoughts of action, and will have the attitude that "it does not matter". It is this total waste of thoughts which causes indolence – though man will not admit that he does waste them. Activity of the body, in the form of *work*, in this civilisation is necessary – man has caused it to be necessary,

61

because he has neglected his Earth. Now he must work to provide food, shelter, and clothing for protection. At present he labours in vain, for he still does not nurture the Earth. Now, all his working is only in a selfish way, for his own personal gain. He labours to produce items of vanity for the cocoon, or to have them around him, or for prestige among his fellow man. *All this for vanity.*

Look at a big-bodied labourer, one who leaves a homeland of fairly fertile ground where all for his needs could be grown, and who goes to another area where he digs in the roads – for money, for vanity.

This is one simple example of how man is in general – how he mis-uses a simple thought to dig. You too, either mis-use your thoughts in a similar way, or ignore many vital ones completely, and so you remain in an uncomfortable position in mind – and ailing in body.

*Exercise* itself is of *no value whatsoever.* No Intelligent being would ever send thoughts to a machine to tell it to perform activities which are, in themselves, useless, or futile. Exercise is mis-use of even the lowest form of Intelligence. Every action thought which is sent to the brain is one with a totally useful purpose behind it, and the cocoon of man would remain in perfect working order, free from the smallest ailment, if each action thought was used – not ignored or mis-used. *Indolence is the ignoring of action thoughts – exercise, the twisting of action thoughts.* Both are stupid and disastrous to the being which is Man.

*Thought activates – Thought is Energy.*

Rheumatism is a very good example of the mis-use of thoughts – and of the penalty that is paid by man for mis-using it.

I refer to Rheumatism in all its stages and varieties, to which the medical profession gives a long list of fancy, foreign-sounding names, concocted from a dead language.

I will use simple words, for it is not *my* intention to hide confusion by baffling everyone else with "science", but merely to give clear understanding to all.

Consider Rheumatism. It starts with an ache, maybe quite slight at first, and most likely in the region of the Spine. The back is prone to aches and pains, especially in the lower part. Or it could be in the area of the rib-cage and also in the limbs.

Those very first aches are messages from your Intelligence, telling you to stop doing whatever action you are doing at the time, and which is against the natural way of the body. For example, you could be lifting heavy objects in your work, or sitting in one position for many hours. You could be typing with your arms and hands held at one angle, or standing at a machine, perhaps bent over a counter, or even standing to attention. All these things are against the natural way of the body, because all of them are a tensing of parts of the body continually.

If you ignore the message of the first twinges or aches, and do not halt and change the position of the body in doings things, or stop doing them altogether, then the aches will be sent again and again. Now the more the aches and pains increase, the more you tend to tense the affected part, the part that received the thought-message from the brain. The nerve-ends make you tense yourself, becoming frightened to move that part much at all. As you do this you are effectively locking the joints, and as this becomes habitual you are developing what are called "Arthritic joints" – merely a more acute form of Rheumatism.

There may be a person with arthritic joints in the hand, caused by tensing them constantly by the action of knitting. But often the person will keep on doing the knitting with the fingers held stiff – locked in one position in order to avoid the pain of moving them. All joints have a natural type of lubricant between the two bone surfaces for ease of movement, and to prevent friction between the two. In the case of the person who holds the hands stiff and knits, or one who "nurses", say, an elbow or wrist in one position, then the lubricant will begin to thicken, go hard against the joints, and eventually break up into particles – "crystalise" as man says.

This is the time when man usually looks for a cure for his Rheumatism, or Arthritis, but it is too late once the joints are locked solid. Action is needed *before* they have a chance to solidify.

Man's higher Intelligence sends him pains in order to make him protect the cocoon. It is the *ignoring* or mis-using, of these pain thoughts which is the danger, and any person who does so, suffers, unnaturally. This way of Rheumatism by mis-use of thought is simple. First an ache – Soul saying to cease what you are doing that is not natural. Secondly, pain – Soul sending a further warning to say "pay attention to this thought". Thirdly, tension – Man holds himself in what he thinks is a way of ease, holding a joint in a protective nursing way, but only tightening the joints of the limbs, or other areas. Lastly, complete locking of the joints, with the break-down of the lubricating fluid.

That is just one example of the many ways in which man ignores the thoughts of his Soul, his higher Intelligence – and suffers for it.

Take an example of a slightly more subtle message, which is so easy to dismiss, and could result in Cataracts of the Eyes.

The first warning thoughts are in the form of hardly-noticeable pieces of "floating" dirt upon the eyes. They may only be faint at first, but if you move your eyeballs suddenly in one direction, the pieces of dirt will "float" in that direction across the vision, in a sort of delayed-action movement.

Oh yes, if you have these particles on the eyes, you will

have noticed them before, many times, because your Intelligence will have sent you the thoughts to notice, without fail. But you probably merely ignored them, as you ignore so many, many thoughts throughout your daily life. If the floating dirt particles are left upon the eyes, without you taking any action, then they will harden into Cataracts. To avoid this is easy. First, wash the eyes with a *weak* solution of salt in water, and then rinse in clean water. Repeat this several times a day, and then you will see better.

The cocoon of man is energised and activated totally by means of thought. Thought controls every minutest particle of the organs, bone, and tissue. It controls every tiniest movement that any part of the body makes – and it provides the energy necessary for that movement.

As far as the body is concerned, the thoughts originate from the implanted, pre-arranged thought-tracks, situated at the Pancreas. From there they are sent along the direct channel to the "Scanner" unit which is situated at the underside of the receiving set – (Brain).

The Scanner unit, by means of the receiving set, is able to constantly view every last dot of a particle of the entire cocoon, for there is a vast and highly intensive network of channels linking the brain to all those parts. By the same means, the receiving set is able to relay thoughts that it receives from the thought tracks, to wherever it requires. This network of thought-sending channels is a set of wormlike threads, sometimes so fine as to be invisible to man of this age. This is what man knows as the "nervous system".

Take out a Cartilage or a ligament or a thread, and the part of the body from which it has been removed ceases to function. It is just as if it had been cut off, from the part where the thread ceases to function.

One particular type of thought which is sent along the nerve-links from the receiving set, and with which man is very much pre-occupied, is *Pain*. Pain, in one form or another, at present dominates man's life. It is not, as you may consider, those senses or feelings which are obviously hurtful – that is only one part of the scale that Pain covers. An itch is pain. When you scratch an itch, you are deliberately causing yourself a type of pain which smothers the irritation of the itch. Therefore the scraping of the skin with the nails must be preferable to the irritation, and so the itch must have been more "painful" to you than the scraping.

There are many degrees of pain. Look at tickling, or caressing, or heat, or cold – these and many more fit into the wide scale of "Pain".

*Pain is the means of Emotion coming into play.* In the absence, in this present civilisation, of any sense of the purpose which would cause man to act in his natural state, emotion is so necessary to cause man to act at all.

But *pain is emotion*, and is required as long as man uses the "wrong" track of thought. The pain-senses of the wrong pathway are used to prod man into action, otherwise he would merely lie down, for he has no other reason for acting, except emotion. It is the worm-like threads, the nerve-links, which carry the emotion of pain along to the relevant part of the body.

Paralysis can be caused either by nerve-junctions being impaired, or it could merely be Soul saying "Rest".

Sleep itself is a form of paralysis, with the body being moved or turned when the thought track sees it necessary – perhaps because pressure on certain parts needs relieving.

Even though it does not appear so to man's present primitive way of viewing by instruments, *all* the nerve-links are *always attached to the brain* – without exception.

Man really must now change his way of blindly accepting all that the medicine men tell him, and consider things more with the *use of his own thoughts*.

When man chooses the wrong track of thought, he chooses emotion. The track sends emotion, in thoughts, to the receiving set, which then sends the emotion round the body to the parts to be affected, via the nerve-links. Notice how emotion causes jerkiness of movement, commonly referred to as nervousness. The Scanner, which constantly acts as the Eye and Ear of the brain, works perfectly until man starts to fret and worry. It is then more difficult to move the Scanner *gently*, and it has to be forced instead of moving smoothly. It moves jerkily.

For example, when a person is doing one job and yet worrying about another thing, then the worrying of the latter jars the functioning of the Scanner for the job in hand, and jerky and clumsy movements result.

Emotion plays havoc with man and with the links to the receiving set – it sets all ajangle. A headache is a jangling of the receiving set, and Migraine is the same, only more severe. It is the Intelligence saying "stop the emotion, use the right track". But mostly man carries on with the worrying and the fretting. Then the eyes can become affected and the stomach upset. If the person continues in this way, then the emotions really get out of control, and he can begin to think he is going "mental".

Really, what was only *concern* to begin with, he allows to grow from an ache to an ailment, maybe a severe one. And so man invents the fallacy of the ailments of "nerves".

Mental institutions are full of those who started out with just a *concern*. If their fellows had employed understanding, and eased the burden of concern for them, instead of handing them over to treatments by drugs and brutality – then there would be no need for any mental institutions.

If only those who perpetrated the brutality realised that Soul arranges it so that they are only being brutal to themselves, to the other members of the same group which

67

make up the one being of a Soulpart. If only the brutal ones would realise this and assist their selves in the form of their fellow man. It is only because man does not *care to understand* his fellow man that mental institutions exist.

If wanton destruction of a large proportion of the brains of man is not to be allowed to grow out of all control – then the outrageous behaviour of the medical men, in tampering with the brain, must be brought into the open. They see tiny movements from time to time, and claim this or that is occurring, and build up wild theories on the basis of those assumptions – but they can never see the movement of the *Force of Life* within man.

So outrageous now are the electrical shock waves which they employ to shock out nerve coils from the head. This barbaric practice can and does permanently damage the "brain-cells" of the victim. Their Soul only permits that they do this to others of the same group – in fact to themselves, divisions of themselves, the one being. They pay dearly for what they do – there is no escape possible.

The medicine men of this age have no true concept of the brain, of its purpose, its functioning. They do not even realise that it is merely a receiving set for thoughts – most even believe that thoughts are made in the brain itself. Such ignorance from those who bestow upon themselves such high-sounding titles! The outrageous behaviour of these people has filled the mental hospitals of the world, yet even now, most of these cases can, *with gentle treatment*, become better persons.

Your Neurologists should aim for gentleness and caring, instead of drugs and brutality. Know that outrageous treatment of your (real) selves leads you towards the Universe of the Wise One. If you do not believe, or do not want to believe, what I say, then I advise you to take careful note of your dreams, from this day on. If even this does not provide enough proof for you – then pay close attention to your waking time too. It is better to reach your destination, when you leave this Earth, in a good way – for this is your last chance.

Now, take careful note of how the cocoon is, using the eyes you have and the thoughts your Higher Intelligence sends, to view the things that I speak of.

To all of man I say – *Pain is unnecessary. Disregard of thought causes pain* to come about.

Man had better be aware, in the days ahead, that Pain is for many a weary year to come, in a more intensified form, unless he changes to a better way. The choice, as always, is his.

*   *   *   *   *

The cocoon of man – by that I mean *your* body – is a machine. It is a machine designed and created by a vast, superior Intelligence. It is no ornament – but a machine built for a specific task, to be performed in a specific way.

Vast Intelligence, by definition, is not stupid. Nor was the Intelligence which designed the environment in which man was placed. It was an Intelligence which foresaw all possible ways in which the surroundings, in which the machine was placed, might change over the ages. Therefore I state that each and every last part of that machine serves an important purpose, which is essential to the total well-being of the whole machine – even though this may not appear so to those ignorant of the true workings of the body.

There are *no* spare parts, or superflous pieces hanging about inside the body. There are *no* extra, useless odds and ends cluttering up the insides of this magnificent machine. To say so would be utterly stupid. All parts, every organ – whether Pump, Liver, Tonsils, Kidneys, Appendix, etc., etc. – all are placed there for a specific purpose. To remove any one of them does far more harm to the machine as a whole than ever it does good – no matter how the "experts" may try to prove and fend.

Let me tell you a small story to illustrate just what I mean. In one of the vast, thick jungle areas of the Earth, some supplies were being delivered to a town not far from the shores of the sea, where there were roads and some modern petrol vehicles. These supplies had been taken by aeroplane and were to be dropped by parachute – this being the simplest method. But some items of that cargo were dropped a long way off target, by accident, and landed in a jungle clearing, just near to a native village. These supplies included an open motor vehicle of the "land-rover" type, and a large supply of petrol, in containers.

After a period of time, the vehicle and supplies were discovered by the natives of the area. At first they were afraid of it, and so they attacked it with bows and arrows, but after a while, as it grew more familiar, they began to treat it as a new toy to play with, and to adore it as a new god.

Of course, the Chief of the tribe and the Medicine Man were the ones who had most say in who was allowed to play with the vehicle, and who were to be its priests and guardians. After a few more days, when it was discovered that the vehicle would move on its wheels when pushed, then a daily ritual was established, whereby the Chief would ride backwards and forwards around the village, seated in the vehicle, whilst the Medicine Man walked in front and a team of his helpers pushed from behind.

An enjoyable time was had by all, until one day the Chief whilst playing with the controls accidentally pulled on the hand brake, without realising what he was doing. The vehicle was jammed it seemed, and no matter how much the pushers pushed, and the Medicine Man chanted, it would no longer move, for neither the Medicine Man nor his helpers knew the real purpose of any of the controls of the vehicle –

even though they pretended to have great knowledge of the wonder machine, in order to impress the rest of the tribe.

Now there had been a similar sort of trouble before, at a time when the Chief had leaned on the brake pedal. No one had connected this random movement with the jamming of the wheels. So the Medicine Man had started chopping at the vehicle with his axe, hoping to make it go. The Chief had been so surprised that he had taken his foot off the pedal, and the vehicle had become free once again. The Medicine Man had been loudly cheered, and was now regarded as an "expert" on the workings of the vehicle. He was presented with a special white robe to celebrate this.

But this time, when the brake lever was applied, he hacked away at the vehicle and still it did not move. So as not to lose his prestige, the Medicine Man declared that the god of the vehicle was tired and had demanded that it was rested for seven days. His words were accepted without question, for as in many tribes, the post of priest as well as doctor fell to the lot of the Medicine Man.

During the week of "rest" of the wonder vehicle, the Medicine Man and his helpers, using a little more finesse than before, examined it more thoroughly and discovered that some items (brake-shoes) were clamped on the wheels, stopping them from turning, *they looked no further*, and called for a big ceremony on the seventh day. The Medicine Man told an admiring crowd that he had been inspired to know the cause of the hold-up, and would now perform the operation to free it.

He took his axe and, one by one, he chopped off all the brake-shoes from the vehicle. They were ceremonially cast into the fire and, amid more cheering, the Medicine Man proclaimed, in his proven capacity as "chief vehicle expert", that the brakes did not serve any useful purpose and should never have been there in the first place, as they only caused the vehicle to stop working.

After that resounding success, followed by unprecedented tribal honours bestowed upon him and his helpers, the Medicine Man really got into his stride.

When the Chief bumped his knee badly on the gear lever as he happily bounced from seat to seat of the vehicle, the Medicine Man immediately solved the problem by chopping off the gear lever with his ceremonial axe, and caste it into the fire declaring it to be of no use. *Everyone believed him without question*, because no one could *see* any obvious use for it – and anyway, who would *dare* question such an expert.

When the windscreen got so dirty that it became difficult to see through, the Medicine Man was by that time so skilled and practiced in the use of his axe, that he did not stop to consider that he could *clean the glass* – he wielded his magical axe, and the problem disappeared in no time at all.

In a short time the vehicle was in a terrible condition – uncared for in the correct way, left out in the jungle rains and burning sun. Not many of the controls were intact, and the axe had taken its toll at random.

So many internal parts had been destroyed and cast into the ceremonial fire, as being of no use to the machine. Some of the tribe believed that the wonder machine had built itself up by an accident of nature (sort of "evolved"), whilst others thought that the original unknown designer must have been just a little bit more stupid than they were to put in all those unnecessary, harmful parts.

The ceremonial fire was always set going by use of the petrol from the containers. *No one suspected that the fuel that they squandered had any connection with the machine they abused.*

And so it remains to this day.

If, one day, a traveller from the civilised world, where the motor vehicle was made, came along to explain to them how they were mis-using the vehicle, and how there was still just time to salvage it, and to make it go again in the way intended by its manufacturer – do you think that they would listen to him, and try to put matters right? Do you think that they would even consider his words? Or, would their blind trust in the Medicine Man and his helpers make them *afraid to listen*, to query, to think for themselves?

You of mankind are that primitive tribe. I am that traveller. Will you open your mind to my words? I leave you to choose.

*       *       *       *       *

*Sugar is poisonous!* Not the raw cane sugar as it grows in the fields, but processed sugar – granulated, refined, polished, and so on – as you buy it in your shops. It destroys certain vital organs within your body. Slowly, yes – but with the certainty of a rat gnawing through a piece of cheese.

Food satisfies the workings of the body – if it is the correct food, the natural food. It attends to the glands and all other organs, and ensures their correct function. Intelligence made the organs so as to deal in a most efficient manner with the proper food intake, to process it, sift, filter, concentrate and Output it.

In a healthy body, all the necessary juices are on hand ready to break down and separate the items taken in. But it is essential that the *natural* items are taken in – and *only* the natural items. Otherwise the body begins to deteriorate.

Consider one of those organs which help to keep the machine in good working order, but which can be considerably impared by harmful intake of substance – the Liver.

The Liver is a means of "purifying" the fluid which is carried all round the body, through the veins and tissues, by the action of the Pump. It changes it from a thick blood-like fluid to a finer water-like fluid. The Liver filters, and rejects that part of the fluid which has already travelled round the body and become cloying. These sticky particles which thicken the fluid are

73

taken out and put into the excretia – but only in minute quantities.

If you examine the excretia carefully, you will notice that it contains tiny blood like particles. At some times there will be far more than at others.

Sometimes the colour of the Output itself will be much darker than at other times. This could be because of certain strongly coloured foods, such as gravy-browning and other dyes. But it could also be because the *Liver* is overloaded with impurities – for example, alcohol, or an excess of sugar.

Sugar is useless to the Liver, as potatoes and rice are useless to the tubes (of the intestines). *Sugar is absolutely useless to any part of the body*. But whereas rice and potatoes, even though they normally clog the tubes become harmless if copious amounts of fluid are drunk after eating – sugar is positively harmful and *actually destroys the Liver*.

Alcohol, sugar and honey when eaten in large quantities damage the Liver action.

Vegetables, fruit and wheat are all very good for the cocoon, but cabbage is good for all the organs, and should never be left out of your regular intake. Nuts are intended for birds and are indigestible to man, but in small quantities will not harm the organs, including the Liver.

Starchy foods are not harmful in any way to the functioning of the machine, and will definitely *not* serve to make you fat, even when very much of them is eaten, *providing* that plenty of drinks are taken *after*, not during, each meal. If you allow them to clog the tubes, then you experience fattening around the base, a swelling in the region of the belly.

*Sugar does not give the body energy in any way.* Neither does Honey – this is strictly for the Bees. In collecting the Honey from flowers the Bees take it in through the mouth, and store it in a sack at the base of the head (having first eaten their fill). When they arrive back at the hive, they put out the Honey once more through the mouth into specially prepared cells. Their summer's work at collecting has to last them all the winter through.

Why be greedy? You have so much of the types of food that were intended for your cocoon, so why take the only natural food that another has, and has worked hard to obtain?

*Your greed is poisoning you* – slowly – and sometimes very rapidly.

* * * * *

Your body is a living machine. Such is its formation and function that it needs constant renewal, constant nourishment. It does not do this for itself, but instead it has within it an army of tiny machines, which do the job for it.

This massive work-force of minute machines is already working in the cocoon at birth. They last the lifetime of the cocoon, if they are not destroyed or taken from the body by some outside force. These machines do not "breed" or grow in numbers at all, but enough are resident within the body at birth to take proper care of every millimetre of flesh, bone, and organs during the whole of its life span. They keep it in tip-top condition, as long as the cocoon is allowed to live in the natural way.

Each single one of these millions of machines knows exactly what to do, what is required of it in all circumstances, because they are *all controlled directly by thought from the cocoon's receiving set.*

Even though they do not "feed" on the body, it is true that they do live on their host, and it is in that sense, and not for any harmful reason, that I call them "*Parasites*".

Your cocoon could not live without these Parasites. They are positioned in every single part, from your eyeballs to your toenails.

They pamper the body. They clean it, nourish it, heal it, protect it. If you are wise you will cherish them, and allow them at all times to get on with their job of keeping the cocoon in an ideal condition – without interference.

*Food* which is eaten by mouth *does not nourish the body* in any way. It merely serves as raw material for processing by the machinery, and Outputting, to nourish the soil and produce Power for the Soul of the Universe.

The body grows in size, and is nurtured by the substances which it takes in from the "air" about it, the "atmosphere". The atmosphere around you is not merely made up of a few gases, but literally millions of differing substances, the vast majority of which man's instruments cannot even detect.

Certain of these substances, which are necessary for the nourishment of the tissues, are drawn into the body *through the pores of the skin*. If you look very carefully you will observe that there is a hair growing in each and every pore of the body. Even on the palms of the hands there are hairs growing within the pores, although with constant use the friction against objects has worn them down to below the level of the surface of the skin. Nevertheless, every pore does have a hair, and it is by means of this hair that the substance is drawn into the tissue, for it forms a hollow tube especially for this purpose.

I say again that every single item, shape, and characteristic of the cocoon is there for a specific purpose, and not accidentally – even a hair.

At the base of each hair, within the pore, there is a Parasite. It is this tireless little machine which draws in the required substances from the atmosphere, when they are needed, and passes them on to feed the tissues with. The body expands from without – not from the "food" man puts within.

Man reverses everything, in his way of thinking, from what it is in reality. And little wonder, when be bases a whole string of reasoning, of theories upon a wrong assumption. In this case, man's experts look at the problem of fatness, and as a first step they examine the food that he eats very carefully, to see how they can control the body-bulk. But they have started off by basing everything on an *assumption*. They *assume*, because they *see* that man takes in substance through the mouth, and do *not see* substance being taken in in any other way, that the obvious must be so – without question.

As usual, and as I have just explained to you, they are wrong – and so all their theories regarding the control of fatness, body bulk, are also wrong. Did not man see that the Earth was flat, in one age, and that the sun went round the Earth? And did not all the "experts" of the day base all their theories on those "facts"?

Man has been and still is, so mis-led by his scientists and medicine men, that he must reverse his ideas in all those ways of looking at things. Then he will be on the right track towards seeing things as they really are.

It is the "Duplicate" thought track which decides if a person is to be fat or thin. The Track sends the signals to the receiving set, the receiving set is constantly sending out thought signals which control the body Parasites, and it is the Parasites which draw in the body building substances from the atmosphere, and manipulate them to add them to the tissue of the cocoon.

In this respect, I am not referring to ailments, such as expanding bowels etc. This is such a very common ailment, as the tubes of the intestines are very pliable, and any blockage or part blockage will easily cause them to swell considerably as matter collects within them. This is caused by mixing animal products with your foods, or especially by eating the dead bodies of the animals themselves. The consequent swelling of the belly is not an increase in body bulk, but a clogging up of alien matter within.

The mixing of vegetation foods is, of course, quite different, and will not produce swelling, but only gases in the stomach, which are expelled through the intestines or the mouth. Quite harmless although a cause of discomfort.

Starving the body of food can cause the machinery to malfunction, and the tissues to begin to "waste" away, or it may cause the body to swell with air. Long periods in between food intakes can also cause the swelling with air – this is very common among would-be slimmers.

*　　*　　*　　*　　*

Man is a killer – in person or by proxy.

Many nations spend almost half of their collected taxes on preparation for killing man. Man plays and enjoys himself killing fellow animal beings, and calls it sport. Man is carnivorous – an unreasoning habitual killer.

Over three million years ago, other beings, different from man, were sent to Earth to help man to fulfill his task. The men of those times killed him and ate his body. They kept some of the beings alive, to have off-spring – so that man could have a supply of alien bodies to eat. The beings, on the whole, did not retaliate against their killers or jailers. They were not equipped for that function. They succumbed. The killers were in control. Today, the descendants of those killers are still in control, are still killers. The alien beings who came to help still exist, in horrific conditions. They are called, in this age, *"animals"*. Such is their payment meted out by man.

Over these hundreds of thousands of years, man has ill-treated the beings who came to help him, with extreme cruelty and contempt, and has feasted off their corpses. All this man has done free from fear of any punishment, any reprisals. He even makes his invented Gods condone such barbarity, and even invents religious ritual killings.

But does he really escape "scot-free" with his cannibalistic ways against his fellow beings. No, he certainly does not! Little does he realise it, but man is paying a very high price indeed. *When man eats the dead bodies of animals — he is eating Cancer.*

He is taking in alien Parasites which naturally inhabit the tissue and organs of the animal – just as man has his own Parasites. But there is a vast difference between your own "friendly" Parasites and the alien ones from another body, another species. The aliens cannot in any way be "killed" by heat, cooking, or freezing. They are machines and man would have to destroy the flesh in order to destroy them. They live on when the flesh is taken into your body. Then, upon finding themselves in alien territory, they commence to attack the organs and tissues of the body.

*All the diseases of man are caused by these alien Parasites.*

They can attack any of the organs, or the tissue or the bones, and not just in the ways which man's experts regard as Cancer. If careful inspection were made, it would be observed that all other "eating away" of flesh and organs, all eruptions, internal and external – is in fact *the same Cancer*.

The size and form of the alien Parasites may vary greatly, according to the part of the body of the animal they were intended to nurture – just as man's are. But basically, they are the same. Tuberculosis is Cancer, Leukemia is Cancer, a boil on the neck is Cancer, Leprosy is Cancer – even a small pimple on the face.

All of these are caused by eating the bodies of animals, birds and insects (*not fishes*) – and also any animal produce such as milk, butter, and so on.

Most of the Parasites are passed out of the body in the Output, but a few may remain each time animals or animal produce are eaten. They manage to cling to the organs which the food passes through and so outward towards the outer skin. The lower organs are most vulnerable – stomach, kidney, pancreas, intestines, and so on. They do not breed, but accumulate steadily as more of them are eaten, or drunk.

Do not remain in any doubt whatsoever – *all who eat animal corpses or produce pay dearly for doing so.*

Not only do you harm your personal selves through greed, but you inflict Cancerous ways on to tiny, helpless babies – the ones you should be caring for, in an Intelligent way. Immediately after birth, in many cases, the natural milk of the mother is withheld, and instead the baby is fed on the milk of other beings – *containing Cancer Parasites* – much in the same way as he will be force-fed with indoctrination very shortly after, instead of being allowed his *natural* way. From the birth of man, an intensive campaign is begun for the destruction of his body and his mind – perpetrated by his fellow man.

When medicine men find someone has a diseased part (Cancer), and they cut it out and throw it away (a futile action), they mostly give the victim more alien Parasites to eat as soon as he is capable of taking in food once again. The victim consumes his portion of Cancerous bodies and his poisons willingly, for he has been indoctrinated into thinking that he must consume a certain quantity of fancy medical names in order to live – names such as "protein", "calorie", "vitamin", "glucose", etc., etc. – although he has neither *seen* these items for himself, nor does he *know* what they really are.

Cocoons of man, animal, bird and insect are made up of soil – they are soil. All vegetation is soil, wood is soil, rocks are soil, iron is soil, wool is soil – all in differing forms. All is alive, though man of this age has not yet learned how to detect the life in all these variations of soil.

The top layer of the Earth's surface in which things grow is a soil which is teeming with countless billions of tiny machines. Their purpose is to break down constantly all the substances of the Earth, and all fresh amounts of substance added to it, such as dead bodies of beings, Output, etc. You could say that these minute machines are "programmed" to do this.

Certain numbers of these machines are allocated to each cocoon of man and animal when it is formed. The "programming" is set aside by thought impulses from the receiving set of the being, which then has complete control over the machines, which are then used to nurture and maintain the cocoon – Parasites I call them.

There is no difference between Parasites in the body and those in the soil of the Earth – only their function is different. All during the life of their host body, the Parasites act according to specific instructions issued by the brain, but once the brain "dies" and stops sending signals – then the Parasites revert to their automatic, programmed way.

Immediately they begin to make their way out of the host body, breaking it down in the process. *This is called "decay"*, and every cocoon begins to decay *immediately* upon death. If placed directly in soil, then other Parasites help in the process, which is then much quicker.

It is important to understand that when an animal is killed, the Parasites within it immediately begin to break down the tissue and to find a way out of the body back to the soil of the Earth. But if a part of that animal flesh is taken into the cocoon of man – then those Parasites within it, which are not eliminated along with the Output, cling to whichever organ or tissue they can – and *begin the process of breaking down (decaying) that tissue just as if it were the dead body of their original animal host*. Two things prevent the immediate decay of the body which has eaten the dead flesh. Firstly, *most* of the Parasites are ejected with the Output. Secondly, the consumer's body has an army of millions of Parasites of its own, which act to prevent the alien Parasites from doing much damage – at first.

81

If your child has eaten animal bodies or "dairy" produce so far, then be pleased when he has an outbreak of chicken pox or measles, or skin rash of one form or another. This is merely the child's own Parasites' way of ejecting many thousands of alien Parasites from the body. It is a massive cleansing process, to give the child another chance to begin again with a cleansed body. All emissions of foreign matter from the skin should be allowed to take place freely. All the whitish pus you see being pushed out of the body, is alien Parasites. They are harmless once out, unless they are licked or taken in again by mouth.

Never try to suppress their ejection or take drugs which prevent this taking place. Let the "disease" play itself out in this respect. *The body was in great need of it.*

This subject of Parasites and Cancers may bring up such questions as – "Why do some people who eat a lot of meat, etc., never (seem) to get Cancer or have much illness?". Or "Why don't meat-eating animals get Cancer?". I answer these questions simply and clearly in another place.

Things which are not *familiar*, easily recognisable, which cannot be placed within the pattern you have built up to fit everything – these things bring unease, a kind of fear even. When man sees anything, he must be able to "place" it. He must be able to give a label to each person that he encounters. If not, then suspicion. If therefore, you feel uneasy at some of the things that I tell you, suspicious of who I say I am, then you are reacting quite normally, as the rest of man. Normally – but not naturally! You have been indoctrinated into habitually closing your mind, against all new ideas, against people who are not as you have been told you are.

The ones who rule your minds – your experts and educators – have a vested interest in seeing that you accept all that they tell you, and reject all that comes from another source – *even your own thoughts.*

Once they lose the right to think for you, then they lose the power they have over you, and with it their prestige and wealth. Would an astronomer ever consider any theory put forward by an unimportant member of the public? Would a medical doctor ever consider suggestions put forward by a "lay" person? Would a judge listen respectfully if you suggested he may be uncaring to sentence a person to death or a lifetime in a cell?

Of course not! It is highly probable that you would find yourself ignored in the first case, struck off the doctor's list in the second, and behind bars in the third. What is more, you would find yourself ridiculed and ostracised by those around you – merely because you put forward *your own thoughts* in an unacceptable way.

Man in general, and experts in particular, are closed minded. "Do not dare to think outside of these lines of guidance laid down for you by your ancestors, and your betters of today" – this is the way you have been educated, indoctrinated. Even the members of the professions themselves are so taught.

"Keep a closed mind, be suspicious and hostile towards ideas we have not taught you, and shun men who are dangerous enough to put forward new ideas without our permission and approval".

Well, now! I am guilty of all these "crimes" against the arrogant ones, who would make you prisoners in mind, who wish to keep the whole of man in a mental straight-jacket. I *am* different – because I am not of man. The *facts* I put forward are disturbing – because they are Truth, and therefore strange to man. It will take a person of *courage* to consider all I put to him in an unbiased, unafraid way. It will take a person who is trying to *open his mind* to Truth, to really listen to my words. It will mean exercising your free choice which your have previously handed over to your educational, scientific, and religious leaders, in order to put my way into practice.

Do you have the courage to do this? Upon your answer depends your glory or your annihilation.

Mankind is in dire need of new leaders now – those who lead from the front by stepping forward and *doing* what is right, not telling others what *they* should be doing. The leaders of this new age of enlightenment, which is upon you now, will not be from the ranks of the over-educated, unless they unlearn the rubbish they have imbibed, nor from the ranks of the scientists and experts, unless they completely reverse their way. They will not be from amongst leaders of religions, unless they turn to Truth and stop pretence.

The new leaders of man will be from amongst the ranks of the ordinary men and women – those of courage and open mind, those who *dared* to believe they were part of the mightly Soul of this Universe, and to know that they did have a purpose in life, and were determined to find it and put it into operation. Are you among them? Come, step forward, leader of men! If you do, you will never have need to fear again, for you will be able to draw upon the Intelligence of the Universe to guide you. Of one thing you can always be certain – Soul looks after its own.

I point the way for you to go now. It is a way that is safe and sure – a way of health of body, of no ailments. I point the safe and sure way to peace of mind, to the solving of *all* your problems and worries. It is simple and uncomplicated. It costs nothing. There is no risk, nothing to lose.

Even if, for instance, you have eaten animal and its products all your life up till now, you can prevent damaging outbreaks of Cancer and allow your own Parasites to push the alien Parasites from your body – merely by stopping eating more animal foods. Even if some part of you is already being destroyed by Cancer – you can ensure freedom from pain in the future, by strictly leaving animal alone. You cannot die one second before the time that you yourself planned to go home, in any case. Only suicides do that.

Follow my words and you will *prove to yourself* that you are indeed one with the Soul of this Universe, that you can be super-Intelligent – happy in mind and body, and setting out on the road to *true* evolution of Self.

I give you some more basic information about your body and mind so that you have a true, clear understanding of the machine that is you. Once you have read and understood my words you will have a greater knowledge of the purpose and functioning of the body machine than any medicine man of today. Once you apply it, you will be far wiser. You will have no need of "experts" in any field – your own vast Intelligence is waiting to guide you.

Look around at your Medicine Men – they have illnesses, diseases, deformities, fatness problems, drink problems, etc., just the same as all the rest of man. Look at your "brain-ologists" – they are just as unhappy, worried, nervous, with just as high a suicide rate, as the rest of man.

Look at your religious leaders – see the arguing and fighting amongst them and their sects, how they cling to material items – see that none of them have found their true selves. They also suffer from ill health, problems and mental illnesses – just as the rest of man.

As I have said before, surely you would not go to a down-and- out bankrupt for advice on how to run a successful business? Or perhaps you would – if he was a clever enough confidence trickster, who pretended he knew all.

Be aware – come alive! Let your common-sense at least, set you on the road to using pure thought, pure Intelligence. Your continued existence depends upon it. The proofs and benefits of turning to your own Soul way will become apparent almost immediately you begin to practice the way – not when you are religiously dead.

Now let us go further with the understanding of the body machine.

Some science fiction writers have already visualised a radical change coming about in the world, whereby each person gets his just desserts naturally, without the need for deliberate interference from any other of man. But they did not realise that this has always been the case, although man of this civilisation has been too stupid to realise it. He just has not taken the trouble to observe. Look for yourself.

Emotions, mis-use of thought, causes many afflictions. The jobs you work at, your way of life, may cause many more. See the pollution of your environment that you suffer from. See how the greed and hatreds of Nations causes it to suffer the agonies of wars. See how what you kill and eat gives you disease and Cancers. The state where you reap the reward of all you think and do has been with you for a long time.

When someone is involved in a personal disaster, and he says "Why me?" – then he would do well to look at his past *thoughts and actions* in an honest way. Then he would no longer say "Why me?" – he would know.

Pluck a hair, from any part of the body. Look at the base of the hair and see the bulb-like swelling at the end, a whitish colour. You are looking at a Parasite. It has attached itself to the base of the tube, down which it draws the substance from the air. It need not continually draw in substances – it depends upon how much nourishment or expansion is required by that area of the body. Some areas are far more active than others, and therefore require far more nourishment – for example, the brain, which is *always* in a state of activity. Notice the amounts and length of hair which grows upon the head – longer in the case of women (even when

86

both sexes allow it to grow), and extra around the face for men.

If you pluck a hair which has a black speck in the white bulb matter, then you have extracted an alien Parasite, which has taken the place of the original one. It will be slightly larger. In the atmosphere all around you there is dirt. It floats in the air and it settles on objects indoors and out. It very easily gets onto the body and into the pores. If a speck of dirt goes into a pore and is not wiped away, then alien Parasites go towards that spot and gather there. That dirt is Soil.

The alien Parasites are constantly trying to find their way out of the body and back to the soil. When they arrive at a speck of dirt in a pore they stop there and expand on that dirt. Your own Parasites then push the aliens to the surface, in order to oust them completely from the body.

The area then may swell, and become inflamed, and a whitish pus appear at the surface. This is called "festering" by man, but in reality the pus is the Parasites themselves.

Washing does the body no good. Constant washing is definitely harmful. It allows no speck of dirt (soil) to collect in the pores, no Cancerous Parasites to gather there, no opportunity for your own Parasites to oust them from your body.

To wash frequently especially with soap, is not co-operating with the guardians of your cocoon – it is to thwart the natural workings of the body.

First you eat the Cancerous Parasites and give your own Parasites the job of trying to prevent them from attacking the organs and tissue, and breaking it down. Then, when your Parasites work them towards the surface and would push them out – you prevent them from doing so. The body should be cleansed by rubbing a light oil over it and wiping it off again. The oil would attract minute particles of soil to adhere

87

to the pores, and the aliens would gather there where necessary.

Also, washing kills the natural oils of the skin, causes sweating and unpleasant smells, and causes the flesh to wrinkle and decay more quickly than necessary. The worst effect of all of washing the skin constantly, is to spoil what the pores take in to *sustain the tissue*.

Notice what happens sometimes if a person who is working or playing in the garden has an open wound, or cuts himself. He can get what is called a very serious infection – "from the soil", your experts tell you. Now there is no such thing as an accident – even a cut or an open sore – and this can be made to occur at the part of the body where there was an urgent need to push out Cancerous Parasites. So it was arranged that the "accident" occurred, that the soil entered the wound, your Parasites got busy, the wound became inflamed and festered, and the alien Parasites were ousted. Unless, of course, your medical man gave you drugs or injected you with more alien Parasites, to prevent this natural cleansing process from occurring.

Another way to restrict the intake of nourishment to the tissues is to wear tight clothing. Articles such as girdles and tight belts prevent the Parasites from functioning (because of the pressure), so that even when sustenance is taken in by other areas of unrestricted skin and passed along – as does happen – still the flesh cannot be cared for in the correct way. It wrinkles and sags and becomes ugly – instead of remaining supple and healthy.

When girdles and corsets are worn to press in a "fatty" area of the body, then a bulge must occur, either on the outside, next to the area pressed in – or on the inside of the cocoon. When this occurs, pressure is put upon organs of the machine, and can cause serious damage.

It is futile to eat wrongly and cause the intestines, for

example, to swell within the belly, whilst compressing them from outside, and further restricting the passage of Output through the tubes.

Hair plays such a vital part in the functioning of the machine which is the body, and yet man regards it as merely an adornment, or else a nuisance. Apart from hair being a means of nourishing and expanding the body, it also serves another purpose – protection. In this civilisation, because of the bad condition of the Earth, and the hostile climatic conditions that man has brought upon himself, it has been necessary for him to labour in order to obtain food to survive, and in labouring need protection of body.

It was intended that the male tend the fields and gather the food – that the female bear children, care for them and for her fellows, gently, and prepare what the male gathered for the sustenance of all.

The head is one of the most vital parts of the body and therefore needs greatest protection. Firstly because it houses the receiving set, and secondly because the mouth takes in the food, the necessary raw material for the machine. The beard of the male was so necessary as well as the hair of the head.

The woman, in her natural way not needing to constantly face the elements, does not need facial hair – except the fine down of the pores which is always there. The hair of the head naturally falls to cover the face as well as the back of the head when necessary.

Apart from producing Power for the Soul of the Universe, man's main task was to plant, grow and use the soil in a good way. Man should use his Intelligence to capacity at all stages, especially in the production of the *natural* food for both himself and for women and children.

As things are today in cities, with most men working in factories and offices, the growing of the beard is not so important, but I point out that it would be most beneficial for each man to *begin* to grow a beard. If he were to let it grow for two or three weeks, it would give his own Parasites in that area a chance to push out any alien. Parasites that had gathered in the tissue in the region of the mouth, where they first have contact with the body when the animal product is eaten. Allow the hairs to grow and the skin to erupt. You may see many white heads appear on the swellings. This pus (alien Parasites) can be shaved off or allowed to come out in another way. Do nothing to prevent it from happening, and be glad that more Cancer has left your body.

An item which concerns women more than men is eyebrows. They serve a very valuable purpose to the eyes, and are most essential. It is the height of stupidity to pluck the eyebrows, and can impair the sight, sometimes seriously. Once you understand the purpose of hair, you will see why.

In the womb of the mother, the baby body grows and expands in size and bulk. It does not eat, take in any food through the mouth. There is a tube which links the baby body to the mother. Therefore, *assume* the medical men, it is obvious that food goes along this tube and "feeds" the baby and causes it to expand.

*Obvious – but wrong.*

Once again your doctor experts glance at something, without really examining it and using higher Intelligence, and proclaim the obvious, as if they know – when all the time they are mistaken and should be looking in the reverse direction.

*All* expansion of body bulk is drawn from the surrounding environment through the pores of the skin. The unborn baby is no exception. Substances are drawn along the hairs and into the body from the fluid in which it lies. A childs body within the womb does not need "feeding" in order to grow. It is not yet a living being. If it were having food put into it, as it does from the time it becomes "alive" at birth, then where is the Output it produces whilst in the womb?

It is so necessary to look at all things using your natural Intelligence – *your own thoughts* – and you will soon see just *how* the experts, whom you have allowed to do your thinking for you, are completely on the wrong track, in so many ways. *It is imperative, if man is to survive, that he begins to think for himself,* and has the courage to state his findings, and question strongly the theories which are fashionable in "professional" circles today.

In this present age it is fashionable to "be concerned". Heads of Nations "express grave concern" over the fact, say, that other Nations have more weapons for killing than they have. Politicians "view with grave concern" the Economic situation, or the rise in violence amongst their subjects. Individuals must show concern over accidents or misfortunes occurring to relatives or acquaintances. You are supposed to be concerned over your children's welfare and education, about a friend's health, about the security of the people you feel responsible for. Concern is a highly respectable and desirable quality in modern society. *But concern is another word for "worry",* fear for the future of self and others. And not only is it unpleasant and useless – *worry is wrong.*

If you worry, become concerned, over anything at all, then you have no confidence in your Self, your own Soul – or, if you are superstitious even in your own particular god. You Trust neither.

Worry is the cause of many ailments of the body and mind – from Rheumatism to Insanity. Concern for self and for others, if they are not in the conditions that *you* think that they ought to be in, is utterly selfish, and is helping to destroy the person who nurses such an emotion.

91

Loss of hair is mainly caused through worry, both gradual baldness and the sudden loss of hair on the head or under the arms. This is merely your Intelligence saying to you – "stop your worrying, stop wanting to change things to the way *you* want them to be – stop being so selfish and change your way".

You will have had many smaller warnings first, to try to get you to change, but at last the receiving set decides on drastic action, and may decide to affect the body in a variety of different ways, according to what you planned to put on your thought track. Loss of hair on the head is a way of hurting you in the area of your vanity, as such great importance, in this age, is placed upon washing, cutting and gluing the hair in place.

Worry cripples the body, lines the face, balds the head, deranges the mind, and upsets the smooth workings of the organs.

Let no one tell you that you *ought* to be concerned over anything on this Earth, even the death of another. Always keep in mind that everyone gets exactly what they deserve and no one can alter that fact.

Remember that all that happens to you is for your benefit, if only you will see the value in it and use it. The same applies to others.

Everyone has his Soul to look after him, to put to him just what is best for him. To *pretend* to be concerned, to *show* concern, it to be a hypocrite. To be always calm and unaffected enables you to care for others in the correct way – it is the road to peace of mind.

*It is wrong to worry!*

When a baby is born it is equipped for living. It can move its limbs, consume the correct food, and it can clutch things. If left to roam free, in an area of flat but soft ground, it will gradually roll about and then crawl, and finally walk –

without any help from any other being. *It is natural.* It merely needs some slight attention, in supplying it with food and putting its Output into the soil.

Very soon it will be able to do even those two things for itself, if the food and soil are placed to hand. It will be perfectly happy and content with the situation, for it will have constant communication with its own Higher Intelligence.

A child has to be *taught* to want things – to want toys, colour, noise, attention, sugary foods. It has to be taught to want to pull and push, and shout and play – to try to *play better than* other children.

When you teach it to want to do all these things, you are *giving* the child nothing – but merely creating false wants and desires which it will not be able to have fulfilled all the time. You are therefore, creating within the child, an emptiness for much of its time. You are taking from it contentment, peace of mind – the very things that you yourself are striving for. You are distracting it from communication with its own Intelligence. In fact, you are merely indoctrinating it in exactly the same ways that you were indoctrinated. Yet you do not realise it, as you take the child from its natural happy way.

If you had courage to withstand the reproof of your friends and relations, and the threats of your professional advisors, you could enable your child to grow up at one with Universal Intelligence, his own Soul. You could allow your child to grow as a person inspired – a genius you might say. But not as a "prodigy" usually is – advanced in one field, one talent, and often lacking in other ways – but natural and balanced and highly advanced in all ways of Intelligence and well being of body.

You could, with a little patience, by allowing your child to grow up *naturally*, free from forced indoctrination, be the cause of bringing forward one of the great inspired world leaders of this new generation.

It is simple, trouble-free – with no risk involved in any possible way of harm to the child. Quite the contrary, in fact. You would be eliminating all danger of disease and illness, physical and mental, all suffering and unhappiness during the whole of the life of the child. As it grew older, of course, the child would have free choice to continue in the natural way of High Intelligence or not. Free choice must always be available to all.

It is simple. First, ensure that the baby, from the moment of birth, is allowed to cry itself out without any attempt to stop it from doing so, either by coddling or stuffing things into its mouth. One hour should be sufficient for this to happen. Then the child should be fed naturally, from the breast of its mother. Not by the clock, but when it indicates that it is hungry. It should not take in any food from any other being, milk to begin with, and meat and animal produce later. In other words – feed it no alien Parasites.

Give it no sugars or artificial foods – only pure vegetables and fruits and wheat foods, etc. At no time allow it to have drugs or chemicals or injections of Parasites.

If fed properly, it will Output almost immediately after feeding. It is simple to place it on or above a quantity of soil and cover the Output immediately. Very soon the baby will learn to do so for itself.

Keep the child in a warm place, on a flat, soft area of ground – free from clothes if possible – or with only very loose, light clothing, if not.

Lastly, leave the child to have a life of peace and quiet, unmolested by yourself, or family or friends. The baby is a being come on to the Earth to do a task – not a plaything, a toy, something to show off to others, or to boost your own ego. Treat it as such. You do not own it – it has merely entrusted itself to your care.

Constantly picking up the child, goo-gooing, pulling faces and waving things in front of its eyes – all this is utterly stupid, and exceedingly cruel and harmful to the child. It is utter selfishness, and in no way for the benefit of the child.

You have a choice, to force it to grow up with all the ailments and problems, confusions and ignorance of life and Soul, that you yourself have had – or to allow it to grow into an inspired being that will be outstanding among men, one with a deep understanding of the Universe, of this Earth, of man and his problems. You will have the credit and the glory of having been a pioneer in this way – one of a group of pioneers needed to bring forward the future leaders of mankind, for the benefit of mankind.

*Babies are born without muscles.* They have the ability to move their limbs, and to grasp things with their hands – but they have no muscles.

If they were allowed to develop naturally, without being pushed into playing at pushing and pulling, banging and striving, wrestling and struggling, then they would grow without ever forming muscles, or ever have need of them. No one needs muscles, and they only appear through mis-use of the body.

Throughout all the tissue of the body, there is a very intensive network of worm-like threads, which are the fine nerve linkages with the receiving set. It is the energy impulses through these linkages which cause movements of the body. It is a very delicate and sensitive system which man spoils. He may start, even as a small child, by lifting things, small at first, then heavier and heavier items, until the tissue around the nerve thread has been pummelled and stretched and pressed so much that it hardens. In time, with continued mis-treatment of straining and jolting, the tissue becomes distended, insensitive, bulging under the skin. It is with pride that man calls it – muscle.

There is, of course, internal muscle and external muscle. The first only shows as swellings beneath the skin, the second you call segs or callouses, and they appear on the hands and feet mainly – but basically they are the same.

If anyone should tell you that muscle is essential in order for man to do the work necessary in life – do not believe it. Would he say that corns and callouses were necessary in order to walk efficiently upon the feet, or segs necessary in order to work skilfully with the hands? Man was intended to use Intelligence and skill to perform all the tasks necessary – not brute force. The ordinary undamaged tissue functions quite adequately for all necessary purposes.

Sometimes a person will pull or strain or jolt too hard, and then the hardened tissue will wrench itself off the wire-like thread, the nerve link to the brain. It is called a "torn-muscle" and can be accompanied by severe pain. Man deserves it to be severe, for he has impaired the way of the tissues receiving instructions and energy impulses from the receiving set. Even as it was, the muscle was paralysed tissue, lumped together in a damaged condition.

The modern Adonis, the Mr. Universe of today, is so much admired by the ladies, so envied by other males, so vain in the love of his own body – he is merely one who has worked so hard to destroy many areas of tissue of his own cocoon. The resulting muscles have little or no means of receiving correctly from the Intelligence.

It is surely true to say that – *Muscles have no Brains*.

The body of man is made up of three different arrangements of substances. Flesh (or tissue) is as soil. With the naked eye, it appears quite different, but if man had a way of magnifying both sufficiently he would see how this is so. Flesh is soil. It came from the soil of the Earth. The Parasites which nurture it are the same as the Parasites of the soil, but under different instructions and control. The flesh goes back into the soil eventually.

But flesh contains one substance that is not of the soil, one which is implanted within it at the formation of the cell, which is to be the body, in the womb of the mother, one which it is arranged to withdraw at the precise moment that the cocoon ceases to be of further use to the Soulpart – at the moment that the thought is withdrawn from the cocoon, and it "dies". This special substance is that which maintains the *shape* of the flesh, against all outside pressures and surrounding substances. It is *Malgum*.

Flesh is made up of soil plus Malgum.

Bone is made up of soil plus certain substances from the atmosphere: the air around. Notice that, if buried in the Earth, bone takes far longer to disintegrate than if left on the surface of the ground. Flesh disintegrates very rapidly when placed directly into the soil. It reverts to its other way of being, with the help of Parasites. Bone is made much harder, and only gradually does it release its "air" substances into the atmosphere.

In this age, to burn the body after use is by far the best method of disposal.

The third part of the cocoon, which has yet a different composition of substances, is the machinery – the internal organs of the body. As the function of these items of Power-making machinery is to process vegetation, which is soil, then they must produce juices which break down that form of soil. If the organs themselves were composed merely of soil-substances, then they too would break down and disintegrate. Therefore, the organs of the body contain properties found in neither bone nor flesh. They are quite distinctive.

Only the flesh contains Malgum, for that has to contend

with the natural action of outside substances, and still retain the shape of the body, whereas the bone and organs are well protected inside the covering of flesh.

Let us look closely at the *bones*. Look at any part of any bone, in a very careful way. It is made up of minute particles which cling together, interlocking, in a very strong way. Between these particles run lots of wire-like *"Probes"*, through every tiniest section of the bone. These Probes contain fluid, and they go all the way through each bone, including the Marrow, in every direction. Bone must stand up to many knocks and jars, and the fluid contained in the Probes lubricates it and keeps it from snapping apart, or from disintegrating in its brittleness.

The Probes are attached in certain ways to veins which permeate the tissues, and these veins in turn are attached to arteries, which carry the body fluid (blood) around the entire cocoon – through the Pump and then to the Liver. Observation of the character and colour of body fluid before and after it passes through the Liver, will show that the Liver is a filtering sponge. Other organs have an outer casing which is harder, more solid than the inside substance, but the Liver is different. It is soft, spongy and pliable throughout. It must be so, for the purpose of filtering. If it is brought from the body into the air, then a harder skin will form, which it does not have when functioning normally.

Man, in his present primitive condition, looks at the veins and yet does not make out their workings, any more than his recent forefathers, could make out what caused the agitation in boiling water when they looked into the pot. How much less, even, do they understand the workings of the much finer Probes within the bones. The arrogance of man, with his science experts, is boundless – especially in the way in which he imagines he is so sophisticated and knowledgeable, when in reality he is so primitive. Man's first step towards wisdom would be to acknowledge and admit openly his ignorance and primitive status.

Man of today is Primitive – make no mistake about that – in spite of all the medals, honours, and fancy titles he bestows upon himself. If he is to gain understanding and knowledge of himself and his Universe, then he must be willing to start to learn from scratch. A self-styled know-all condemns himself to remain stuck with his own ignorance.

Probes are *not* veins. They are similar, in that they carry fluid as the veins do, but their function is different. The Probes carry fluid to the centre part of the Bone, in order to keep this area moist. As the fluid goes along the Probe, from the outside to the centre, it is thickened by what is contained within the Probes, so that by the time that it arrives at the centre cavity, where is stored the Marrow, then it is in jelly-like form.

Because of this process, the Marrow is able to fulfil two functions – to nurture the bone, and to lubricate the joints of the bones. At the end of each bone, at the place of the joining with another, there is a small opening. It is through this opening that a *minute* quantity of jelly-like fluid is ejected from time to time, when required. This is the lubricant which enables each bone to move against the other, without scraping or wearing down, smoothly and easily – also, *painlessly*.

Rheumatism is an indication that thoughts have been mis-used, that the Liver has been neglected. Neglect of the Liver means neglect of what passes through the Liver, by means of the Arteries, through the Veins in the tissue, the probes in the bones. It causes therefore, neglect to the Marrow, and a lack of the necessary lubricant to smooth the movement of the joints. All is so simple to those who are *willing* to see.

Rheumatism is not an Intelligent condition to be in.

It is totally unnecessary. All that man has to do is to stop eating alien Parasites and an excess of sugar. Vegetation, fruit, and a little fish, can provide a varied, pleasant and wholesome diet – without ever the need to feel hunger, monotony, or unsatisfied. After eating in a wholesome way for the period of about a year, even the worst Arthritic case will have improved sufficiently to be able to move all the joints. The body is designed like that – able always to put itself into a good condition, if it is nurtured properly.

That is the function of your *own* Parasites. The reverse is the function of the alien ones.

Damaging the Liver can cause other ailments besides Rheumatism/Arthritis. Varicose veins, for example. The body fluid (blood) goes in a pure, fine condition from the Liver to the outer skin, and then back again. It goes via the wide Arteries through narrower veins, then very fine veins to the surface skin. It collects all the impurities as it does so, and takes them back with it towards the Pump. It goes also to the Probes of the bones, although only a tiny fraction of fluid is taken though the Probes now and then. The Pump serves as filter – rather, it smooths out the impurity-laden consistency of the blood, which then goes to the Liver. Here it is filtered even more, and the impurities are taken out of the fluid system. The fluid is then, once again, fine, clear, free-flowing.

All this takes place, of course, when the organs are in a natural, healthy condition. If, however, the Liver is not able to refine the thickened blood, because of neglect, then many impurities remain and *they clog the fine veins*. They become what man calls "varicose veins".

The Pump gently draws the impure, thickened blood towards it, and as it passes through the cavity it filters it, and smooths out the "lumpy" particles – ready to be further filtered and extracted by the Liver. If the Pump is faulty, this can also damage the Liver and the veins.

Man imagines that it is food particles which are carried in the bloodstream from the stomach, and are then filtered by the heart. Once again, the obvious is not always consistent with reality. *Assumption* is not correct.

Hairs of the skin take in particles from the air to nurture the tissue, bone, and organs of the body. Both the polluted particles from the atmosphere, and the useless *used* particles from the tissue etc., form the impurities which the Liver is expected to filter and expel into the Output. It is rather like a waste collection and disposal system.

It is simple, not complex. There is no mystery about the body. Of course, it can be made to *appear* to be complex, by those who are ignorant of its workings, whilst pretending to know much – or by those whose interests are best served by deliberately keeping others ignorant of the little they know themselves.

Mostly, your Medicine Men treat you in a high-handed manner, as if you had no right to know what they were doing to your body, or as if you were a small child, too weak-minded to understand why they are giving you this drug, or why they throw that organ away – or even refuse to tell you what is contained in the "medicine" they give you. Be aware.

Neglecting care of the Liver also damages the Pump. Intake of alien Parasites can cause the Liver to decay, intake of excess sugar and alcohol causes it to atrophy. When the Liver hardens, the fluid by-passes it, and impure fluid is circulated again round to the Pump. The Pump cannot cope with this and becomes impaired. Man concentrates on trying to treat the Pump – as if it were more important. Neither one can function without the other.

In some countries, it is thought that salt is harmful to the functioning of the stomach. This is not so – but it is the *Iodine* that is mixed with the salt before it reaches the shops, that helps destroy the Pump. The Iodine in your salt (to make it easy flowing) eats away the part of the tubes of the Pump which smooth out the blood particles – the burrs on the inside of the tubes. *Iodine can halt the functioning of the Pump.* A damaged Pump, in turn, can damage the Liver.

Additives to food and drink, forced on to the often unsuspecting populous by manufacturers and so-called "health" authorities, *always* have a destructive affect upon the body – in spite of any good that they are supposed to do. Consider Iodine in salt, Flouride in your water, etc., etc. You have no way of knowing what you eat, unless you make sure that you insist on eating, at all times, only what is intended for the cocoon. Man camouflages so much.

*Any chemicals consumed*, no matter what the excuse or pretext given, *always help to destroy the body of man*. They are *always* more harmful than any possible good that they may *appear* to do.

In the same way that Probes inter-lace the particles of the bone – so the minute veins inter-lace the tissues. In fact, it is these tiny *veins which hold together the tissues*. The veins have minute burrs on the outside, and it is to these that the substances of the tissues adhere.

The veins are so minute and so close together that when you cut a piece of flesh, it appears that the blood comes from the flesh itself, as if the flesh is soaked in blood. This is not the case. Even in a one inch cut you can sever dozens of tiny veins. If man cared to use one type of microscope which he already possesses, he would *see* the clinging burrs on the outside of these veins. The veins "feed" the tissues, after having taken substance from the pores, and fluid from the Liver. At the thousands of junctions in the network of veins within the tissues, there are small one-way valves, through which the moisturising fluid (not blood) is pushed. It is not a continual flow, but is fed to the tissues when required.

Your Medical Men tell you that you have in your bloodstream, red cells and white cells, but he does not tell you *what they are* – Because he does not know! He is content to give them a fancy name (such as "corpuscules"), which implies that he must know all about them. Yet he doesn't!

I will tell you. The red "cells" are some of your own Parasites, part of that vast army of tiny machines which patrol, protect, and nurture your body. The white "cells" are Cancer Parasites, Alien machines which are programmed to "attack" and break down all tissue and organs that they encounter, until they find their way back into the soil. They are present because you have eaten them with your food.

As long as the white Cancer cells are kept moving, are prevented from attaching themselves to any part of the vein tissue, then they can do no harm. It is the function of your own (red) Parasites to keep the aliens moving, until they can push them out of the body in some way, but two conditions can prevent them from doing so. Either the Cancer Parasites become too numerous for your own Parasites to handle, or blockages in the veins allow them to attach themselves to these parts, and start "eating" through the tissue. Cancer then breaks out.

Leukemia is caused by constant flesh eating, whereby you can end up with far more alien "cells" in the blood. It has been overrun by the "enemy".

You know the Cause – You know the Cure!

Is the taste of Cancer, as you chew it, so pleasant that you cannot resist eating it? If so, I have no desire to take away your free choice. Up to now, when you ate the Cancer Parasites you did so unknowingly. If you continue to do so now, you do it with your eyes wide open.

I do not speak out to decry, to condemn the Medical

profession. That would serve no purpose, for all get exactly as they deserve, no matter what words are spoken by others – they planned it themselves. I speak out solely to enlighten man to the dangers of "medicine", to enable him to eradicate the apparent need for it, to show him how to prevent all disease.

There are many honourable men and women who have been trapped into conforming to, and using the ideas and theories of, their controllers, instead of using their own thoughts. There are many of that profession who would take a better way if it were pointed out to them, as it has been now.

I have no wish to take away the livelihood of the men of Medicine. On the contrary, I urge them to take up a job of work which is beneficial to mankind. Are there not many such jobs available, such as tilling the land, planting crops, etc.?

If those of the Medical profession really do wish to devote their lives to the greater benefit of man, as they claim, now is the time to show the world that they are sincere. Let them not live off the diseases and ailments of their fellow men, but rather help to produce the wholesome natural food, which can rid him of all his diseases. Do they really need to be so particular, that they only accept work which carries title and prestige with it, as well as excess wealth?

The production of vegetation food is so important.

Very soon, because of drastic changes which are about to occur upon this Earth, man will be scrabbling to grow food on every inch of land he can. But will it be too late? Mass starvation is near. I do not prophesy, I do not threaten – I state a fact.

Soon money will be of no value, if food is not available. Hoarding resources at the expense of others is the height of stupidity. All who store wealth will be depriving *themselves* of food in the near future. It is futile for a rich man to hoard, when his underlings are starving, or even the ones who would produce the food for those underlings.

When a man's body machine runs down because of lack of food intake, then it would be useless for Soul to place there energy thoughts. Machines cannot use energy when the works are clogged through lack of use.

When those who would produce food at source, those close to the land, are starving, and their machines are running down – then they will have no energy or will to grow food for the rich even, very shortly. The rich may panic and start pouring out their wealth upon the producers of food – too late. It takes time to care for the land in a good way, to nurture the crops. Over night it cannot be done.

Money, resources should be invested in growing food *now*. Time grows short. Vast areas of many lands are unused for food growing. Much lies under weed – Grass. Where grass grows – so can wheat, or other grain.

In some countries, millions are unemployed, but provided with money, millions are in useless professions, millions work in factories churning out ornaments and useless goods. Millions more are employed making weapons of destruction to be used on their fellow man. At the same time millions of acres of ground lie wasting, idle. *This is truly insanity* on a world-wide scale.

It is essential to your survival to invest money in food growing *now*. The winter of hunger draws near. Open your eyes and see for yourself.

The rich ones who hoard uselessly – money, resources, or *land* – and deprive others of the means of food, will find that they cannot eat jewels, nor will bank notes satisfy their hunger. How will they feel when they may be among the last survivors to witness the downfall of all of man – to see mankind annihilated before their eyes – because of *their greed*?

# CHAPTER FIVE

In this chapter are set out ways in which you, mankind, can assist yourselves. Ways of value are given to you – ways which you can use for your own and your neighbour's benefit. Look now towards the way of a new child. You are coming into a new way of life yourselves – even the oldest among you. You have to change, one way or another, for nothing ever stays as it is. *Change now is imminent.*

There is no longer any need for old ones to sit with thoughts of failure in life, with thoughts of faded dreams – nor for young ones to wonder what on Earth they are going to do with their lives which they have in front of them. I am here to give you hope, and a purpose in life you have never dreamed of before, that can turn your life, here and now, into a fascinating, enjoyable, satisfying existence – such an existence as will set you on the first rung of the ladder of evolving, immediately you leave this Earth.

I am here to tell you who you are in reality – not that frail or crumbling body which you now inhabit, but a being of Power and Intelligence, a being of wonder, if you could only see yourself now as you really are, and one of such potential greatness as to make you gasp, merely at the thought of it.

Ignore what the leaders of religion tell you – that you are, away from this Earth, the same as you appear to be here – that you are a miserable sinner, a plaything of some God or other, made to please him and adore him.

I say you are not – *and I know*, for I am of the Core of the Central Mass of Power, the Intelligence that runs through all life.

I say to you – get up off your knees, stop your crawling and grovelling, your whining and your chanting. Stop humiliating yourself, and so insulting the wondrous being of which you are a part – the Soul of this Universe.

Have the dignity of a *true man*, one who was made to walk upon two legs, not crawl upon four – leave that to the priests and those in fancy dress, who are arrogant enough to do it. Let them play, until they learn better ways. You have a right to *know* who you are, *be* who you are. Let no one take it from you.

If you are young, you now have a life of wonder to look forward to – for this really is the dawn of the age of Enlightenment. The years of the Wondrous One have already started. You have so many powers of mind and body as yet untouched, undiscovered even. You can begin now, today, to open your mind to the flow of pure Intelligence from the Soul of this Universe.

The world is, in reality, your oyster. The Soul of this Universe needs leaders now, those who are not afraid to handle the Power and Intelligence that will flow through them for the benefit of the rest of mankind, if they will only make the effort to open that channel of the mind through which it must come.

You have that channel – all of man has that same channel. How to open it and use it is simplicity itself. Up to now you have had no chance of doing so, for those who led you on this Earth were in ignorance of the fact themselves. They ensured that it was well and truly closed at birth, in their efforts to make you what they themselves had become.

If you have the courage to tune in to your own Soul thought-track, then you will discover, automatically and naturally, without any experts telling you, that you have such powers in your hands and in your vision as you never dreamt of. You will be able to use those powers with Intelligence that no man can teach you. You will come to *know* that your brain is only a receiving set, for you will receive such understanding of yourself, of mankind, of your Universe, that could never be created or stored within that lump of matter you call brain.

Once you are in direct link with the Universal Intelligence you will never again grovel before idols and imaginary gods, and kiss the hands of arrogant so-called agents of those gods. You will know and see Truth.

Soul now scans the Earth to see who are worthy, who have sufficient courage and openness of mind to be *Leaders of Men*.

Changes are indeed about to happen on a world-wide scale. Old ways are about to be swept away – new ideas, revolutionary inventions are about to be put forward in every field of life. Scholars and scientists of today are going to be exposed as the *primitives* they are, by the wonders about to span the planet. Leaders are needed to put forward those ideas, to lead man out of this age of darkness and ignorance.

You can be one of those leaders, for the benefit of your fellow man.

And after, when you leave this Earth, you will have earned a great leap forward in evolving high into the realms of Soul of this Universe.

The Centre of Power of the Universe draws to itself those of courage and dignity, of Caring and Intelligence – like itself – and not the crawlers and the whiners, who debase themselves for what they imagine to be personal gain.

When I say that the way to open your channel to Pure Intelligence is simple, I mean just that – *simple*.

There is no need to sit for hours meditating and concentrating. No need for placing the body in unnatural positions, or murmuring meaningless sounds or words. The only requirement is that you be *natural* – not what you have come to regard as *normal* or *habitual*, for that is merely the result of a lifetime of indoctrination, but naturally being what you are.

You are *not a body* – this is merely a cocoon for housing Power-making machinery. You are *not a personality* or character – this is merely an accumulation of contaminated ways of feeling and thinking, a pattern of emotions and set reactions acquired along the way. You are *not the brain* or mind – this is a receiving set for directing the actions of the cocoon, nothing more. You are the being who controls, or should control, all those parts in the pursuit of your reason for being.

You are a Part of the Mighty Soul of this Universe, you are a magnificent being whilst away from this Earth and in your natural state. You are able to tap the Source of Power and Pure Intelligence of which you are a part. Away from this Earth you glow, you shine, you have a vast understanding of how all is on Earth. If you fail to complete your task on Earth and have to come back again, you dread the idea of coming once more into such a state of ignorance and decay of mind and body, of such hatred and greed and violence. Abortions in childbirth are because so many of you fail in courage at the last moment before you are born again onto this Earth.

In Soul, *you are great*. If you were allowed to come to Earth in your true state, you would dazzle the eyes of man with your brilliance, your Power, and your Intelligence. Not only this, but you are a Part of the Being which formed the Universe itself.

Let no one tell you that you are a miserable sinner, a cur to be whipped according to the whims of Gods, made to grovel and beg forgiveness for being lowly. I tell you – *you are great*, even on Earth, when you begin to be your natural Self. Start using your whole potential now. It would be stupid to use only one tenth of your brain when you could use the whole, stupid to use one part of a thousandth of your Intelligence, when you could use it to capacity – stupid to make do with a crumb, when you could have the whole loaf. *You can*. Let me tell you how.

First, put your cocoon in order, so that it will serve you well, so that the machinery will function as intended. It was never intended to have aches and pains, illnesses and diseases. Pain was never necessary – why not abolish it from your life? You can put your cocoon in order by eating the correct foods. *No animal* or animal products – these contain Cancer Parasites (as do vaccinations). *No drugs. No chemicals* added to foods, where this can be avoided. Vegetables, fruits and a little fish will provide an ample and varied diet. This is the natural way.

Overcome harmful emotions – these will destroy your health and peace of mind. Start with *Intolerance* – which is allowing yourself to be adversely affected by the words or actions of others – and allow them free choice to go their own way, as long as they do not encroach upon your purpose in life. *Worry* is the next most harmful emotion, and there is only one way to abolish this – that is by replacing it with *trust in your own Soul*, that everything is arranged for your benefit, if you will only look for the value in each situation, no matter what. There is no other way to rid yourself of worry, and therefore to acquire peace of mind. If you sincerely begin to follow the way of your Soul, it will take care of everything for you in a good way.

Intolerance, worry, and *greed* – the scourge of man.

Each emotion which you manage to overcome will automatically be replaced by a new sense. It will bring about an acute awareness of your fellow man – his feelings and ways of thought – and an understanding of the Universe around you. When you rid yourself of emotions, you do not become less alive. Just the reverse, for you develop the senses which enable you to live a more alert, enjoyable, and satisfying life than ever before. You become a better person, more useful to your fellows and to your Self – for emotions are the violences of thought which block you from using your Higher Intelligence.

The next item is to *use your own thoughts*.

In Soul, you are the equal of all your fellow beings, in Power and Intelligence. You will become far more wise than the self-styled "experts" and authorities on various subjects, if only you will allow your own Higher Intelligence to come through. You cannot do this if you *allow others to do your thinking for you*. The only way to use the Wisdom of the Universe – is to use it, *direct*.

Question all you see around you – the traditions, the rituals, the taboos, religions and inhibitions. Look into the "intelligence" of the fashionable "moralities" of the day, of your corner of the Earth. Look into the system of forcible indoctrination in your land – education it is called. Does it help and train man to fulfil his purpose on this Earth – or just the reverse?

But when you look – look with an *open mind*. Do not merely judge what you see according to the principles you have gathered during life – but examine the value of the principles according to each *new* idea. Man loves what is familiar, even when it is bad he clings to it. But he rejects, usually out of hand, the unfamiliar.

To be *free in thought*, means to be free from the fear of using your *own* thoughts. Any other way, because of fear of what others may think or do, is the way of a slave. Which are you going to be?

In the same way that you require freedom of thought – free choice to go the way your own thoughts direct you, freedom to follow your purpose in life – so you should allow the same freedom to all others, including family, especially family.

To presume that *you* know what is best for another when you cannot know what his Soul requires of him, what he planned for himself before he came to Earth – that is the height of arrogance. To fail to fulfil your own task in life – that is a tragedy, but to prevent another from completing his – that is evil. Allow others to lead their own lives, with a wife, husband, son or daughter, etc. They too, have a Soul which takes care of them exactly as they deserve – exactly as they planned, according to the path they take *of their own free choice*. Do not try to choose for them, you cannot do so.

It is your duty to your Self to develop your own potential to the full. What is called "instinct" in animals, could be called "inspiration" in man. Allow yourself to be inspired – but allow your child to take that way also.

Man herds children together in indoctrination centres, as if they were cattle. He daily puts them in pens, forces them to sit in small seats for many hours whilst he force-feeds them with valueless facts – just as he puts hens in battery cages and force-feeds them in unnatural conditions – to make them produce what *he* thinks is valuable to *him*. No one can be forced to do what is not on their value or valueless track. It is equivalent to mentally torturing helpless children, to try to force them and pressurise them into remembering and "memorising" the thoughts and ideas of others. No such thing as memory – no such thing either, as escaping paying in full for unnecessary torture of helpless fellow beings, whether they be cattle, battery hens, or man-children. Indoctrinators beware.

Look afresh into what you do – and how you do it. Herding helpless children and forcing them to do your will for endless numbers of hours – this is called *discipline* when backed by "authority", *bullying* when it is not backed by authority.

One point to keep in mind and to bring to the fore whenever you are tempted to act against another, or interfere with the free choice of another, whether within the conventions and rules of Society or not, is this – You, Soulpart, are a being which divided itself up into several parts before you came to Earth, and it is probable that several parts of your Self are inhabiting different cocoons of man at this moment. You did this in order to give yourself a better chance of fulfilling your task in life. One part of your Self which takes the right path of Caring is sufficient to bring all the other parts of your Self to the same way. Those other parts of you are likely to be around you in your daily life. Your wife, or your mother, *may be you* in reality. Your servant or master could be you. The man you judge or convict, the one you kill in private or in war. The ones you prevent from freely following their own thoughts, their own purpose. Your children or the ones you indoctrinate in schools. The ones you cheat or "do down" in business. The ones you hate or persecute. All or some could be the other parts of the Being, the Soulpart, which is you.

This is just one obvious reason why it is only Intelligent to be *Caring* of your fellows. You are merely caring for your Self.

Consider a group of islands, scattered in the middle of a vast ocean. How differing they can be – one green and fertile, one barren and bare of vegetation: one rich in food and fresh water, one dry and with nothing edible: another large, another small: one beautiful and scenic and another ugly and scarred. What a wild assortment they can be, all within one group. Some you may love to visit or live upon, others you shun and avoid at all costs.

And yet – *all islands are linked below the surface.*

Only the water makes it appear that they are not in reality one mass of land.

Drain off the water and you will *see* that they are one land mass, and know that what you thought of as individual islands were merely the tips of the same piece of substance, poking their way up into another world, another dimension.

So it is with man – in reality all one, but in the dimension that is Earth, seemingly separate individuals. This point, this *fact*, is so very important. Bear it in mind in all that you do, and you will know that *Caring* is the only Intelligent way.

One emotion, which can prevent a person from acting in the way his own thoughts will lead him, is *Fear*. Fear can make a person run away, cower in a corner, pray for mercy, become frantic and insane, or it can paralyse the body and numb the brain. Any one of which will destroy his chance of fulfilling his destiny.

Fear is usually in the form of what man inflicts upon man in his greed and cruelty, and less usually in the form of what man calls "the forces of nature". These objects of fear are real enough, but there are those which can drive a man to stark terror, and grip him for the whole of his life – and these last *do not even exist*. They are the super-natural beings and spirits, invented by religions.

They were invented and used by religious leaders in order that they could rule the ignorant masses by striking fear into them – so that they could then provide "protection" against these spirit beings, for the price of obedience and "support" of the religions in question. The system is similar to that used by many parents of a generation ago, who invented bogeymen to frighten their children into doing as they were told. No difference, except that one implants the fear of bogeymen, the other instils the fear of spirits and devils – and even the "fear of God" – into their victims.

There is danger to the mind and health in thinking that

spirits roam back and forth about the Earth, and yet to many it is a convincing theory. Some even take it as a definite truth. Certain groups of people have gathered together, from various religions, myths and stories of spirits and ghosts and such like, and have made a new religion from that aspect alone. Playing upon the gullibility of man, they create prestige and wealth for themselves by becoming leaders of such a religion.

There are many stories of spirits, which are put about as fact, of ones which guide, and control, give messages, and even come into the body of man – or emerge from the body in the form of "ectoplasm".

Most of these activities and "phenomena" are performed in a way that is deviously sinister – and for good reason. A magician, who openly states that he does tricks to fool his audience, performs his wonders of magic in a bright light, much to the credit of his skill and sleight of hand – but those who trick with intent to deceive *need dim light*.

How easy it is, with the aid of thread to take from and return to the mouth quantities of very fine gossamer-like material – which is supposed to be "ectoplasm". No such thing!

Photographs are produced supposedly showing a smoke-like substance coming from the person, and yet no smoke is detectable in the seance room. Many times have photographic plates been tampered with. Trick photography was the hobby of many persons once – but trickery is far easier to detect today. Still, some "mediums" of spiritualism use this means of faking to convince others of their greatness.

Part of the stock-in-trade of many mediums is the state of "trance". This is said to be a dream like quality whereby the being of the cocoon is supposed to step out of it and stand aside to allow another being to use the body. This is always, in every case, sheer trickery, because of the simple fact that there are *no other beings existing* who could do such a thing.

Again, observe the machinery of man, the way the being functions, and you will see that as a receiving set exists, it must have something to receive. Where from is a mystery to man, who thinks it is, or can be, plucked willy-nilly from the air, or "ether" as it is termed.

Charlatans make the mistake, therefore, of thinking that that "something" received comes from outside of the machine. But in reality, all that a person (cocoon) receives in the way of thoughts or senses, comes from the implanted "tape" within the body. None can interfere with that whether spirit, ghost, goblin, or fairy. And yet, it is supposed that in this "trance" condition, one or more entities attach themselves to the person whilst others pass along messages. How futile!

In order to prevent close scrutiny of their antics, mediums tell searchers into truth, and also their own supporters, that light is dangerous to one who is in a trance – and they therefore, have to work in the dark. Do these supposed spirits, then, live in darkness, that they are afraid of the light of day?

They also say that it can affect their solar-plexus if one touches them or makes a noise, whilst they have control over the audience. This is an excuse to have accomplices stationed nearby to stop others approaching and looking too closely at what is going on. No one on Earth can go into trance, for the track of thought to the receiving set comes from the being's own Soul, his own Source. No other can enter into the receiving set of man – under any circumstances.

Strong thoughts, voices, and even visual impressions may, in rare instances, come to a person – but all comes from within, and it is a matter of how you have arranged your own thought pattern – *up to reading my words*.

I come to assist you to find Truth, but it is something that *you* must find for yourself, *by your own efforts*.

Ideas of hob-goblins, devils, spirits and fairies are implanted in the minds of man from childhood, and man frightens children with ghost stories and such. See how they become a part of man's make-up, and set up a life-long fear of shadows—shadows that rise from the ground where the frames of man are buried, for instance.

So ingrained is this insidious form of indoctrination, that man can become afraid of the rustle of a tree – even in a city.

A shadow, even of yourself upon a wall, may send a shiver of terror through the body. An unsuspecting animal gently walking by at night can be startled by the yell of a fearful one, and then there are two frightened creatures, or sometimes more.

Men use many varieties of ghost and spirit tales to frighten each other – as fantastic as were-wolves and vampire bats, etc. Yes, even the gentlest bat is made to appear a gruesome, bloodsucking monster.

Even certain dreams, which are sent to try to show man how he is, which are intended as lessons to help him, have been turned into "nightmares" by man's unnatural fearful reaction to certain sights.

All due to indoctrination with fear.

Religion contributes largely to the upkeep of those fears. Priests use exorcism to put out from man that which was never there in the first place. Not so long ago they used to cut it out with knives, whilst the victim screamed for mercy he did not receive. Today the torture inflicted is on a mental level – that is still condoned by Society.

No matter what the symptoms which the priests try to cut out or extract by chantings, man cannot take in anything from another source – only what comes from his own thought track. The most common symptoms which priests like to exorcise are those of epilepsy, because it appears the body is under the control of another (sometimes crazed) being. But he cannot exorcise epilepsy – it is more than man is capable of.

Epilepsy only comes when the individual requires use of Soul – not religion. If he did turn to his Soul way, then Intelligence would show him a way to peace of mind – for that is what he lacks. Epilepsy is caused by worry, anxiety, and so on. The victim gets into such a state that a "fit" comes about – for the agony of mind is too great to bear. A little caring and understanding on the part of those close to him would do far more good than a thousand rows of priests in long robes all chanting in unison.

Come, why not take the first step out of this primitive age of phantoms and devils, of spirit trances and religious exorcisms? In this matter you are no more advanced than savages in the jungle. Priests and religious leaders are the played-out figure-heads of an age of dark superstition and stupidity of man. Spiritualists bring disrepute on the way all really is.

If you are one of those who are open-minded enough to believe in the possibility of spirit realms – then why not open it wider and see and understand all about the True Realms of Soul. Many of you are sincere, are searching for Truth, have perhaps discovered that there is something there which comes to you, that is not accountable by conventional, religious or scientific theories. But you have been misled into believing that it comes from without.

See how you can indeed receive guidance and wisdom from your own Soul – from within – *direct*. Prove it to yourself beyond doubt, now. If it is truth you seek, not sensation – then there is no need for dim lights and ghost stories, nor priestly rituals.

What are needed now are strong, sensible, straight-as-a-die people to go amongst man, exploiting in the bright light of day the rich and astounding potential which lies within them – not fakers, hood-winking man with mystery. Mystery is a word which covers ignorance, darkness covers deceit.

* * * * *

Good intentions not fulfilled are useless – weak resolutions futile. Each of man upon this Earth has come with the intention of completing a task in life, and when he returns to his realm he looks merely to see whether or not he succeeded in doing so. He judges himself – but he judges by results, for all the intentions in the world will not Power the Universe. Soul goes only by results – there is no other way.

If Power is produced the Universe expands, the beings evolve until they attain the same exalted state as the Soul of the Universe, raw Power is sent to the Core of the Mass, processed and multiplied, then sent out to be used for the benefit of all.

The making of Power is vital to the continued existence of this Universe and the beings which are man. No matter what else you do or talk about doing upon this Earth, you annihilate yourselves unless you make Power. That is your reason for being. You make Power by allowing the machinery within the cocoon you inhabit to process vegetation food in a good manner, and then by *placing the Output*, the finished product, *into the ground*.

If you do this one simple thing, even if you cannot overcome harmful emotion, it will still be considered that you have fulfilled your task, and everything harmful or evil that you have ever done, *up to the moment of reading my words*, will count for nothing. Such is the dire state of this Universe that your Soul will set aside all that has passed. You can begin afresh from *now*. Soul, of which you are a Part, goes only by results.

Unless man wishes to see the whole of the surface land

of this Earth turned to desert – and soon – then he must put his Output into the ground. Those who laugh will soon see less humour in the situation when starvation strikes *at them*. Those who sit back smugly, hoarding possessions or land unused, should realise that a person can be poor one day and rich the next, or rich one day and a pauper the next. Each one has planned, on his thought tape, what will happen if he takes the wrong track and if he takes the right track – once he has learned of Soul and his purpose on Earth.

This age now is man's last chance to justify his continued existence. He will not be allowed to endanger the rest of the Universes of Soul, merely because of his greed and selfishness. This Universe will be closed in in a flash, at the least sign of danger to other Universes, because of the broken link in the chain of Power which this Universe creates.

But before that moment arrives, Soul is so caring of all, even those who cause a Cancer within it, that it has sent sections of itself to this Earth to give man a chance of turning, of his own free choice, from a way of nil-intelligence, to a way of Highest Intelligence – from viciousness to caring.

Caring for what is one's Self is Intelligence, for it is the only way to survival of Self. You are a part of the Soul of this Universe, of the Universe itself, a part of all Souls, all Universes. *You* are a part of all that is. *To wilfully destroy* anything, is to destroy your Self, is a form of *insanity*. Only Caring is Intelligent.

Soul cares for you, for you are of Soul. The Soul of this Universe has itself decided to take its part *on Earth* in the Plan to help mankind to save itself from annihilation. It is already on this Earth. It occupies the form of a baby, a baby born in the normal way. It entered into the cocoon at birth, as you entered yours. *It is here now*.

Already its indoctrination has begun. It has been born into a highly religious family, and already a barbaric sacrificial operation has been performed upon it – it has been circumcised.

As the boy grows older his pattern of indoctrination will intensify, and the straight-jacket of prejudice and superstition will be placed upon his mind. He will go through all this and more, but he will overcome the imposed folly of man. He will use the right track of thought, he will tap the wisdom of the Universe which is his in his natural state. What is more, he will be in direct link with the Core of the Mass of Power.

He will show to mankind, in all ways, wonders that have never been seen on Earth before, or dreamed of. When he steps forward and sheds the bonds of family and religion and social indoctrination – *then he will shine*. There will be no need to ask who he is. The man will be called Thomas – and known as the Wondrous One. He will have, ranged alongside him, an army of Souls and Soulparts from other Universes. The weapons of that army will be Intelligence in the form of Caring – Caring for Man. Caring to show him the way out of his present ignorance and turmoil – to show him the way to evolve *with dignity*.

Nothing will stand against the Wondrous One and his army for long – but, as always, man will have free choice to listen and follow or to turn away.

The Wondrous One will extend the Caring of Soul to each one of man, as an equal. He will greet you with the words – "You are as I" – *for he really will be you*, and you a part of him.

I do not speak of some vague time in the far distance when you will all be "dead", as you say. I speak of now. *The Wondrous One is here now*. Merely an infant – yes. But one who will begin to dazzle the world by his sixteenth year.

And before this, there are among you now, about to step forward, sections of Soul from outside of this Universe. They have appeared as man in almost every way, but now they begin to throw off the ways of man and show what and who they really are. Each will do what he came to do, and care for man in the way he planned. Wisdom and enlightenment is now to be man's for the taking – if he so chooses that way.

But also, there are now upon this Earth Soulparts who have already completed their task of making Power for this Universe, and who come from the highly evolved realms of Soul. They do not come as the rest of man, to make Power for Soul, but they have a special mission. They are here to assist the Wondrous One and the Soul sections from other Universes, in caring to bring man into a better way. They are here to lead their fellow man to his *true* destiny.

These special Soulparts have within them a strength that the ordinary man and woman does not know, although so far it many not have had a chance to come to the fore. They may have felt a discontent with the way all is in Society, a desire to put things right if only they knew the way. They will have felt a keen desire to help man out of his misery, and perhaps even have tried to do so in their own way and failed.

These special, evolved Soulparts will feel a thrill of hope for mankind when they read these words, a feeling of anticipation, an enthusiasm for all to begin. They will feel a longing to be Part of the Plan, for the starting of a Golden Age. They will feel at one with the author of these words – and it will all be quite natural, for they planned, on their thought track, to feel such a response at the very moment when that Plan was about to begin.

*You*, who read these words, may be one of the Special Ones of mankind. *You* may be, in Reality one of the Highly Evolved ones, who come with a special mission to this Earth.

If you feel that you are such a one, then have no fear of your capability to carry out such a mission – for in Soul you are Great, Magnificent, and it is arranged for all the necessary courage and Intelligence to be placed at your disposal, backed by the Power that you have earned in past ages.

If you feel that you are such a one, *know* within you that you *are* such a one, then step forward and take the place that is rightfully yours, for you were born to lead – at the right moment. You were born to be a Pioneer for Soul, to prepare man for an Age of Wonder – to prepare him for the emergence of the Wondrous One.

The difference between a leader and a follower is that a leader steps forward – *first*.

In Soul, you are as I. If you *dare* to be as I on Earth, then seek me out – but as an equal, believing that you and I are One. Bring me nothing – you have nothing that you can give me. I have all.

Little Island, look, and see that you are in reality the tip of one vast mass of land – of Power, of Intelligence. You and I *are* One.

This is not the end of the book, but the very *beginning of a New Era*.

It is *you* who will write the last chapter ... *make it a glorious one*.

# NEVER BEYOND UNDERSTANDING

## Keith D. Edmunds

You are here on Earth for a definite purpose. You can understand what that purpose is.

Within these pages is information of many ways—ways of thoughts and senses, and how your Universe truly functions as one of many other Universes.

Past, Present and Future are herein.

Ways of putting the mind at ease. Ways of clearing once and for all time, from the face of your Earth the ailments of Man.

Make sure you understand the contents, and be sure to ask if you are in doubt.

# INSPIRATION – IS FOR ALL

## Bill Dawson

How was this Universe formed? What lies outside of this Universe? What is your true purpose on Earth? Where did you come from before you began life on Earth?

What other kinds of Beings exist outside of this World, this Universe?

What kind of a man was Jesus? And was he anti-religious? Is it true that highly Intelligent Beings watch this Earth closely now, ready to communicate? What is the key that will trigger off the unimaginable Powers lying dormant in each of Man? What is the fact, not theory, about other highly-advanced civilisations that existed many thousands of years ago?

Only a man of all times, all places, all ways of life, could answer those questions with authority and certainty. A Being who was present when all those events took place, a Being from outside of this Universe, and yet one who has lived within it.

Just such a Being does exist. Just such a Being relayed the words of Pure Intelligence contained within these pages – through the pen of one who is as you. A Being, to whom no mystery exists, inspired the answers to all of these questions, and many more.

You too, can become a Man Inspired, with a direct link to the Source of all Intelligence – simply. Inspiration is not for the privileged few – Inspiration is for All.

# WOULD YOU BELIEVE AN ALIEN?

## Keith D. Edmunds

I have been here before in many guises, always
with the intention of putting to rights the uncaring
ways of others for their Earth.

But as always, you of man have had to make your
own decision – whether to believe me or not.

In this book I tell you a little of those past times.
Some of you may even recall the action of them.
You would then understand my way.

## "ORISSOR"
*is the way for All*

## Dorothy Fosbrooke

Why cause yourself to have CANCER, or for that matter any sickness whatsoever?

Why ponder over the ways of this Universe? Understand your own Earth and in which Universe it dwells. Everyone can understand what *all* is about.

I say that you can use substance as well as I can – whether you believe me or not is for your to decide.

Everyone on Earth should have free choice to make their own decisions.